TEACHING WRITING IN
MIXED-LANGUAGE
CLASSROOMS

Powerful Writing Strategies for All Students

Joanne Yatvin

New York • Toronto • London • Auckland • Sydney
Mexico City • New Delhi • Hong Kong • Buenos Aires

DEDICATION

For all the young writers whose work appears in this book and their classmates whose work would be here if there had been more space

Credits

The author and the publisher wish to thank those who have generously given permission to use borrowed material:

Page 136: "This Is Just to Say" by William Carlos Williams, from THE COLLECTED POEMS: VOLUME I, 1909-1939 copyright ©1938 by New Directions Publishing Corp. Reprinted by permission of New Directions Publishing Corp.

Editor: Lois Bridges
Production management: Amy Rowe
Cover design: Brian LaRossa
Interior design: LDL Designs
Copy editor: Jennifer DePrima

ISBN-13: 978-0-545-11590-2
ISBN-10: 0-545-11590-6
Copyright © 2009 by Joanne Yatvin
All rights reserved. Published by Scholastic Inc.
Printed in the U.S.A.
1 2 3 4 5 6 7 8 9 10   23   14 13 12 11 10 09

CONTENTS

ACKNOWLEDGMENTS

Although I never expected to be quoting myself, I can think of no better way to acknowledge the people who helped me bring this book to fruition than to repeat what I said in an earlier book: *No writer writes alone. No teacher teaches alone. We are surrounded by a crowd of shadowy mentors, whispering their knowledge in our ears and re-enacting their experience in our mind's eye.*

My most immediate mentors have been seven teachers in high-poverty schools in Portland, Oregon: Emma Harris, Allen Koshewa, Sheryl Lindley, Sharla Sanford, Mary Starrs, Lisa Staver, and Sally Wells. All these teachers bring skill, creativity, perseverance and devotion to the teaching of writing—and everything else—in their mixed-language classrooms. In addition, I want to thank principals Susan Dunn, Heidi Masanuga, and Shane Basset for inspiring their teachers and giving them the freedom to make curricular and instructional decisions in the best interest of their students.

My more removed mentors are the teachers at Crestwood Elementary school in Madison, Wisconsin, where I was principal from 1974 to 1988. Back in the days before standards and testing narrowed the school curriculum and sapped teachers' energies, they developed a school-wide writing program that was revolutionary in its time and is still powerful today.

To identify the early mentors who shaped my understanding of good writing, I have to reach back many years to my time as a graduate student at Rutgers University. My mentors were the professors who assigned the works of Chaucer, Shakespeare, Milton, Pope, Melville and other greats for us to read and then expected us to write about them clearly, succinctly, and without jargon.

Returning to the present, I want to acknowledge three colleagues who read parts of this book while it was in progress and gave me good advice: Pam Perrin, Brett Dillingham, and Allen Koshewa. At the same time I want to acknowledge my editor and friend, Lois Bridges, who is always responsive, supportive and helpful when I call on her, just as a good teacher should be. I also appreciate the respectful and efficient work of my production editor Amy Rowe. As always, my mentor behind the scenes has been my husband, Milton Yatvin, who makes it easy in so many ways for me to lead a writer's life.

What's a Teacher to Do?

All over America English language learners (called ELLs throughout this book) are being educated in regular elementary classrooms. Although some of these children have spent time in bilingual classes before their current placements, and others are now receiving an hour or so a day of English as a second language (ESL) instruction, they still need a lot of support for learning. In oral activities and cooperative learning projects, teachers and classmates give that support by helping ELLs find the information they need, supplying the words they don't know, and accepting their less-than-perfect grammar and usage. Most of the time, easy-to-read books are available in classrooms to provide ELLs with background knowledge about unfamiliar subjects. But when it comes time to write, ELLs, like their native English-speaking classmates, are expected to go it alone, selecting appropriate topics, deciding how best to cover them, and finding the language to express their thinking fully, clearly, and correctly. Often, this is too tall an order for children who have missed out on years of schooling in the ways of American life and its written language. Some children just give up, and some teachers give up, too.

Although the original impetus for writing this book was the situation of ELLs in regular classrooms, I could not ignore the fact that there are other children in the same classrooms who also struggle with writing. That's why I have addressed the needs of native English-speaking students as well as those of ELLs. But above all, this book is for you, their teachers, who must consider all your students when you plan instruction, when you demonstrate and explain new material, and when you identify students who need extra help.

METHODS AND MATERIALS

In my experience, the materials and methods commonly used to teach writing in mixed-language classrooms are inadequate for the breadth and depth of the job students are expected to do. Not only do many commercial programs assume that all children are alike, they also chop writing into its parts and focus far more on the mechanics of spelling, punctuation, and word usage than on the background knowledge and conceptual power every writer needs. While a writing workshop approach offers students more leeway to express their own personalities and interests and more relevant instruction in the form of mini-lessons, it often does not provide them with direct support before or during the writing process. Only after students have made their decisions about a topic and written their first drafts do the teacher and other students step up to give assistance. Traditional writing textbooks offer even less support than the other two approaches, separating instruction from writing altogether. These texts focus on the four standard types of writing, formulas for constructing paragraphs, sentence variation and combination, and exercises in grammar, usage, and punctuation. Students are expected to call up these generalities and transform them into the specifics they need while immersed in writing.

With any of these programs, competent English-speaking students may succeed by drawing on the knowledge and skills they've acquired through their home backgrounds and personal reading, but ELLs and strugglers often do not have enough of these resources to fall back on. Without them and without supportive instruction, they may do no more than put some pedestrian—and, often, unrelated—sentences down on paper. Their finished pieces too often reveal a meager vocabulary, immature and repetitive sentence structure, and a lack of information, thought, and feeling.

DIFFERENCES BETWEEN SPOKEN AND WRITTEN LANGUAGE

Program weaknesses are not the only reasons young writers need support before and during writing. An additional problem is that ELLs and other at-risk students may be more at home with spoken language than written language, which are different in several important ways. Even at the level of literal communication, written language requires complete sentences, names and descriptions of things that the reader cannot see or hear, punctuation to replace missing voice intonation, precise verbs, and more nouns than pronouns. The box on the following page illustrates all of those things with two different language examples representing the same incident. Unfortunately, my example of spoken language is not truly authentic because I can't speak it to you; I have to write it. Still, I think you'll get the idea.

In addition to the differences I've just pointed out, you may have also noticed that my example of written language starts with a participial phrase, producing a sentence structure that is common in writing but almost entirely absent in speech. This is just one stylistic feature that differentiates written language from spoken language. However, the most distinguishing characteristic of written language is coherence. Unlike spontaneous speech, which rambles on, repeats itself, and switches topics randomly, written language is held together by the purposeful organization of words and sentences into paragraphs, sections, and complete entities. Because of its coherence written language has greater power to inform, persuade, and please its recipients than its spoken counterpart.

Spoken language: Look there. Who did that? Was it you?

Written language: Pointing to a puddle of orange juice and a sprinkling of cereal flakes on the kitchen counter, Mom asked Jonathan if he was the culprit.

SUCCESSFUL TEACHING STRATEGIES

The problems inexperienced and disadvantaged writers face are serious instructional issues, and there are no quick and easy solutions. Nevertheless, many teachers are helping their students make significant progress in writing by integrating a variety of supports into their teaching. In this book, I describe several of the most successful teaching strategies I have observed or used myself in classrooms where ELLs and native English speakers were learning together.

At this point, let me say something about the nature of those successful strategies. Almost always, they include "front-loaded" supports, that is, assistance provided to children both before and while they are writing. Good teachers front-load their teaching by building a fund of knowledge I call "context" that includes firsthand experiences, informational sources, visual images, oral explanations, relevant vocabulary and, above all, models of the kind of writing students are expected to do. Teachers also demonstrate how the various parts of that context can be used in the process of writing, guide their students through that process, and provide classroom partners who assume the role of critical listeners.

In identifying supports for writing, I must emphasize that they are always offered as choices, not prescriptions that children must follow. For instance, students are free to take as much or as little from a model as they need, or to ignore it entirely and write on a topic and in a form that are altogether different. This point is important for teachers to understand because many English-speaking students will use only a few of the supports provided, and ELLs will differ in how much they need.

In addition to teaching strategies based on building a context in the classroom, this book includes other strategies that rely on children's own experiences and the language that accompanies them. Those experiences that deal with forms of popular culture, games and sports, interaction with family and friends, features of their own community, travel to other places, and recreational reading are, in themselves, contexts. Because such contexts are more familiar (and less demanding) than school-based literary and academic contexts, students need less teacher support for writing that is grounded in them.

THE ORGANIZATION OF THIS BOOK

In planning this book, I tried several organizing approaches, but ultimately decided to use types of writing as the organizing centers of chapters and include different strategies for primary- and intermediate-level students in every chapter. In addition, the sequence of chapters moves—roughly—from easy writing to difficult writing.

This organizational structure means that it won't be easy to pick and choose the strategies for the grade level you teach or for the types of writing you are most interested in; you are going to have to read—or at least skim—the whole book. But by reading it all, you will better understand the entire range of writing that elementary students should be able to do and the supports they need.

A DILEMMA

I also faced a dilemma in presenting examples of student writing. Although I had plenty of examples for the writing types I intended to cover, not all were written by children in the mixed-language classrooms of high-poverty schools. Many were the work of native English-speaking children from the middle-class school in Wisconsin where I was principal for 12 years. Believing that these examples would serve well as models for writing in your mixed language classroom, I wanted to include them; but I didn't want to misrepresent them. Therefore, all the examples from my Wisconsin school appear without authors' names, and the examples from Oregon schools have the first names of the children who wrote them.

Even though the sources of all examples are now readily identifiable, another problem still remains. The Wisconsin students' writings passed through other hands before they came into mine. I have no way of knowing how much the teachers or the parent volunteers who typed up the writings edited them after students handed them in. Conversely, the writings from Oregon students came to me with little or no editing by adults. As a result, the examples I present in this book make the Wisconsin students look like much better revisers, spellers, and punctuators than the Oregon students, which is probably not true. As you read, please keep in mind that adult editing can make young writers look more mature than they really are.

A WRITING PHILOSOPHY

Finally, I want to be explicit about my philosophy of writing right at the beginning. Although this book is meant to be a concrete, practical guide for teaching writing in mixed-language classrooms, it is based on beliefs I have developed over 50 years as a teacher of children and adolescents, a mentor of teachers, a classroom observer, a lover of literature, and a lifelong writer. Here they are.

1. Writing is more than inscribing letters, words, and sentences. It is the power to communicate knowledge, thought, and feeling through written language.
2. Every form of writing is characterized by rules and conventions originating in a particular culture and developed over time. Overall, writers follow these protocols so that readers can understand their work and feel comfortable with it. What makes a piece of writing original is its content.
3. To be successful at any form of writing, writers first need to become familiar with that form through their reading and teachers' presentations of examples.
4. Teachers need to provide a full range of supports for their students, who, at the elementary level, are writing novices. Students should be free to use as many or as few supports as they need.
5. Learning to write well is a lifelong journey. Each small step taken along the way is a worthy accomplishment.

I hope you will find this philosophy and the teaching strategies and writing examples that have emerged from it easy to use in your mixed-language classrooms and effective for all your students.

CHAPTER 1

A Context for Writing

The central principle of this book is that children's school writing experiences should be embedded in a supportive context. That context can be anything from a social studies unit, school project, or the books of a particular author, to a popular sport, social relationships, or a community problem. The choice hinges on what children are interested in or need to write about at the time. Be aware, however, that I am using the terms "interest" and "need" rather loosely. We can't always expect children to recognize what they want or need and tell us about it. Interest can grow out of something new that the teacher has brought to the attention of the class. Need can grow out of assigned work that inspires children to learn more and communicate their knowledge to others. In short, interests and needs are whatever moves children to write and do it well.

To give children the support they need, a context for writing should be as all-enveloping as you can make it. Context is not a one-shot exposure to a poem, a news article, or a classroom problem, but a cluster of experiences around a theme, made meaningful to children through seeing, hearing, speaking, reading, and thinking about its various facets. Such a context is commonly referred to as "background knowledge," but that term does not do it justice because it does not make clear the amount, variety, and depth of information a child needs to write about an unfamiliar topic. Perhaps the reason personal narrative writing has become so widespread in classrooms is that children's knowledge of their own lives is the one context teachers can count on. Conversely, the reason other types of writing are so rare may be that teachers doubt the sufficiency of students' knowledge of genres and topics beyond their personal experience.

MODELS AS PARTS OF CONTEXT

One important but little-recognized component of any supportive context is written texts that serve as models and springboards for new writing. Because written language differs from spoken language, children who are inexperienced with its forms, styles, conventions, and technical characteristics need the support that experienced writers—professional and amateur, adult and child—give through their finished writings. By examining those writings and using them as the foundation for their own work, children are able to create pieces that others will find meaningful and pleasurable to read.

A HISTORY UNIT AS CONTEXT

To clarify the concept of a supportive context, let me describe two classroom contexts that teachers have used successfully to generate student writing. The first context is a social studies unit called "The Western Movement," which is taught in fourth or fifth grade all over America, and the second is a class field trip. Although many teachers approach the social studies unit through textbooks, the teaching team I observed started with a piece of fiction that they read aloud. They continued by providing students with short informational articles, showing videos of early settlers traveling west, playing music of that time, and taking their classes on a field trip to a history museum where they could see genuine clothes and artifacts from that period of American history. Then, small reading groups read and discussed trade books that were biographies of real settlers or fictional accounts of frontier life. The teacher in the vignette below is a composite of all four teachers on the team.

TRAVELING THE OREGON TRAIL

Jeremy Stone adapted a popular simulation game that has students make choices about what to take with them in their covered wagons, which routes to travel, how to cope with the dangers of the trail, and what to do when food or water runs low. He also found examples of authentic writing from those times, such as posters, newspaper articles, letters to relatives, and diary entries, and shared them with his class.

As the students relived the journey west through simulated experiences, they did a lot of their own writing, pretending to be the original pioneers. Their immediate supports were authentic writings of the past and the trade books they had read. Below are examples of student writings done by these fourth and fifth graders. If some of them look too good to be true, be aware that Mr. Stone allowed students to borrow vocabulary and sentence structures very liberally from the models he presented. These students also had to revise and edit their pieces before their teacher would accept them. Finally, Mr. Stone read every finished piece very carefully, knowing it would be published in a school writing collection.

Signs Posted in Towns Where Pioneers Stopped

FOR SALE

2 oxen

1 iron cooking stove

1 oak rocking chair

WAGON MASTER FOR HIRE

Experienced guide will bring you
 to Oregon safely.

Knows how to talk to Indians

Knows where water holes are

Dedications for Personal Journals

To my dear sister Faith

who gave me help and confidence

all the way

I dedicate this diary

to my Pa who made me feel safe

through all the dangers on this trip.

Gravestone Inscriptions

Here lies Joe Harris

who was shot by Shoshone Indians

1837–1859

Here lies our son

Seth Martin

Died of small pox

March 1852

Warning Signs for Later Wagon Trains

This trail is rough on wagons.

Go through the valley.

This water ain't fit to drink!

Watch out for Indians at the river.

Journal Entries

I opened the door. There stood a man with a horse by his side handing me a letter. Then I found myself crying as it said that Steven's pa was ill in Oregon and needed us to take care of him and the Blacksmith shop. Today, Steven sold our home and store. I reckon it was the saddest thing to see it all go. We told the kids, Mathew and Samantha, about leaving. They thought it was grand.

The days have been busy with excitement but hard decisions of what to bring because we knew we could only bring what the wagon would hold. Things like . . . warm and cool clothes, pots and pans, great-grandfather's hand carved rocker and so on. We had to leave the rest of the furniture. We decided to bring one cow for milk, our dog, Prince, and four oxen to pull the wagon. The rest of the animals were sold.

Our last trek was to say our prayers for a safe journey to Independence, Missouri and to say goodbye to our fellow friends.

Now on to Oregon!

Letter to Relatives Back Home:

My dear brother Sam,

Liza, Gramps and I made the final decision today to head out to Oregon. Liza didn't really want to leave Virginia, but she was outvoted. Gramps and I are just itchin' to see the rest of this country and be a part of a new territory. Might try a little farming there til I can make a living selling dry goods.

We decided to go by train, then by wagon to Independence, Missouri, where the wagon trains head west. Will write again from Independence so you'll know we're okay. Maybe you'll come out west, too.

Your brother,

Tom Bonner

A CLASS FIELD TRIP AS CONTEXT

A different type of context for elementary-level students can be a school situation or event that captures their interest. Understanding the power of motivation, teachers often allow their students to write letters of complaint about cafeteria food or the conditions on the playground during recess. Although this is a valid activity, it is usually a one-shot writing experience with only a limited context to support the young writers. In contrast, I want to describe the context and the writing activities that grew out of a school field trip. The teacher I name is also a composite.

Sarah Aked took her third-grade class to visit a local museum where there was an exhibit on robots. On their tour, the children had a guide who explained how the robots were constructed and programmed. Back at school the children talked about what they had seen, then made a class list of the robots they remembered, with annotations about what each one could do. Then Ms. Aked asked the children to write about what they considered the highlights of the trip. As expected, these pieces focused on visual perceptions and feelings. Below is what one girl wrote:

> Our class went on a field trip on Thursday, January 16th. It was fun on the trip. We saw a lot of things. We saw a show with two robots. One of the robots was named Topo and the other was named RVSX. Topo was operated by a computer. The robots could clean up a room. The robots were neat. I thought it would be a show, but it was a tour. I liked the show and the tour a lot.

Hoping to give the children a clearer idea of how robots worked, Ms. Aked obtained a video about the making of robots. She also had them read an article from a children's magazine. Afterward, the children wanted to make real robots at school. Although the teacher appreciated their enthusiasm, she had to point out that they did not have the tools, materials, or safeguards to work with metal and electricity in the classroom. She suggested instead that they make imitation robots from cardboard boxes and tubes and decorate them with colored paper and aluminum foil. They could make moveable joints by using large brass brads. This project took about two weeks, resulting in robots that resembled animals and people. From Ms. Aked's point of view, a more important result was the robot-related vocabulary that the children assimilated.

Ms. Aked suggested that a further step might be to write programs for their robots. She showed them one she had written for setting a dinner table and tried it out by having a child act out commands one by one, with a real table, plates, and utensils. When the human "robot" became confused at times, the children began to understand how complete and explicit a program had to be. After the teacher made corrections in her program, the human robot was able to set the table correctly.

Now the students felt ready to write their own programs. When their drafts were completed, they tried them out with a partner and then made corrections.

Here is Dan's draft of the program for his robot to do homework:

Go to the coat rack.

Open my backpack.

Take out math packet.

Come to my desk.

Put packet on desk.

Open packet to first page.

Grab a pencil.

Start doing the problems.

Complete the first three pages.

Flip the packet shut.

Put back the pencil.

Thank you.

After watching his program acted out, Dan realized that it did not tell the robot to close his backpack after taking the math packet out, where to get the pencil from, or to put the packet back in the backpack. He added those directions to his final version and felt ready to demonstrate to the whole class.

Since some of the children finished before others, Ms. Aked allowed them to demonstrate their programs with a human robot. Most of these demonstrations showed that there were still flaws in the programs that left the robots not knowing what to do. The demonstrators corrected their programs, and the observers went back to their own unfinished programs on the lookout for similar flaws. Finally, everyone produced a program that worked.

Even after all this work with robots, the children still wanted more, so Ms. Aked suggested that they write stories imagining what their robots could do. Here's Lesley's story:

My robot can walk and talk and has moveable joints. If you touch the red button on his back, it will say "Sorry." If you touch the blue button, it will say "Hi." My robot can play checkers with me because he has a computer in his head. He has electronic eyes so he can watch me sleep at night.

Below is a narrative written by a boy in the class. It is not clear whether his account is totally imaginary or partly true. In any case, his continuing enthusiasm for robots comes through.

The robot Chris, Mike, and I are making is made of an old toy truck, walkie-talkies, 60 spark plugs, and a cord. It can go frontwards and backwards and we made it! It has a light in its head. He can pick up things. He can move in the dark, too.

When the class finally moved on to other interests and the regular curriculum, Ms. Aked felt very satisfied with what they had accomplished. The context she had provided beyond the field trip experience produced a deeper understanding of robots and better writing.

MY STRATEGY

In choosing these two examples as illustrations of how children's writing can be supported through context, I have deliberately relied on situations that can be reproduced in most classrooms. In other words, I am using a strategy similar to the one I am encouraging you to use for teaching ELLs—call up or create familiarity with a theme and provide models of written language to support children as they write.

As you proceed through the types of writing and suggested supports in this book, you will not always find contexts so thoroughly described. I am counting on you, knowledgeable teachers, to search out new contexts or seize existing ones that will be right for you and your students.

CHAPTER 2

Pattern-Based Writing

For children just learning to write, the kinds of patterns that appear in stories, poems, songs, and playground games are a powerful support. Although many children struggle trying to write original pieces of any length and coherence, they can easily use a literary pattern as a framework upon which to hang their own words or as building blocks that can be assembled in different ways to create new patterns. Most patterned pieces are written for young children, but there are also many that appeal to older students and even adults. The verse patterns of traditional songs, such as "Down in the Valley" and "Michael Rowed the Boat Ashore," for example, can be altered by mature writers to make songs that are entirely new.

ELLS AND PATTERNS

The idea behind using patterned writing to support ELLs is that literary patterns are easier for them to see, imitate, and remember than straight prose writing. The fundamental structure of patterned writing stands out because of its repetition. When particular words appear over and over, children remember them. Not only do ELLs readily add these words to their spoken vocabularies, they also remember their meanings, how they are used and, often, how they are spelled. When a pattern has rhyme and rhythm, too, the whole thing sticks in memory.

POSSIBILITIES WITH PATTERNS

Here's one example of what young children could do by imitating the pattern in the popular children's book, *Mary Wore Her Red Dress*, by Merle Peek. The book tells a simple story about animals going to a birthday party in the woods. On each page, one new animal appears. The text names each animal, a prominent article of its clothing, and that article's color, using the same sentence structure and the same rhythm. The page illustrations represent all three text elements visually, giving strong support to beginning readers and ELLs. The book begins—

Mary wore her red dress, red dress, red dress,
Mary wore her red dress all day long.

—and continues with the same pattern throughout.

As an extra enticement, this pattern lends itself to singing or chanting. After a teacher has read the story once or twice, most primary-grade children are able to repeat it orally by relying only on the illustrations. The pattern seems to tickle their ears and tongues, and they like it even better when the teacher encourages them to insert their own names, clothing, and colors, or those of their friends.

Because this story pattern is so appealing and so easily remembered, it makes an excellent support for writing. Young ELLs and struggling writers can follow it all the way through with minimal substitutions or go further by envisioning a different set of events. Here are just two of many possible versions that vary from the original:

Susie carried her lunch box, lunch box, lunch box
Susie carried her lunch box all the way to school.

Sammy tossed his football, football, football,
Sammy tossed his football all afternoon.

Note that the pattern structure remains intact even when the events and objects change, giving ELLs the support of well-formed English sentences while allowing them to use their own experiences and imaginings as the content.

Some Patterned Books

As primary-grade teachers already know, *Mary Wore Her Red Dress* is typical of many patterned books for young children. There are probably hundreds of such books on the market today, many of which have stayed very popular over the years. To help you get started building a collection of patterned books, I have listed a few of the best-known titles below:

It Looks Like Spilled Milk by Charles G. Shaw
What Do You Say, Dear? by Sesyle Joslin
Fortunately by Remy Charlip
Are You My Mother? by P. D. Eastman
The Great Enormous Turnip by Alexei Tolstoy

Bears in the Night by Stan Berenstain and Jan Berenstain

The Very Hungry Caterpillar by Eric Carle

Rosie's Walk by Pat Hutchins

The Little Red Hen Traditional

OLDER STUDENTS' USE OF PATTERNS

At this point you may be wondering whether these simple patterns will appeal to older students. Should teachers use books such as *Mary Wore Her Red Dress* as a support for writing in the intermediate grades? Yes—but not in the same way they would use them with primary-grade children. There are at least two other approaches that support older students' writing. One is to suggest that they create books for younger children based on existing patterned books. There is no reason why sixth graders can't enjoy writing books for kindergartners and first graders in their school. If such a project is presented as an experience in real authorship and preceded by the careful study of several well-written patterned books, students will accept the challenge.

A second approach is to suggest that students use simple patterns in creating their own personal biographies. "All About Me," a commonly taught unit in the intermediate grades, can serve as the context. In their biographies, students could use photographs or drawings of themselves or friends and write patterned text that illustrates some of their activities past and present. Here are two possible examples using the *Mary Wore Her Red Dress* structure:

Laura wore a Badger cap, Badger cap, Badger cap
Laura wore a Badger cap to school yesterday.

Alan got a new haircut, new haircut, new haircut
Alan got a new haircut last Saturday.

ALPHABETICAL PATTERNS

As I mentioned at the beginning of this chapter, playground games are also a good place for finding patterns. One ball-bouncing game that goes way back to my childhood is "A, My Name Is Alice." Here's how I remember the first part:

A, my name is Alice
My husband's name is Arthur
We come from Albuquerque
And we bring back apples

And so on, through the alphabet, with players supplying their own A–Z words (except for Q and X). A player lost her turn if she could not think of an appropriate letter word on each bounce of the ball.

If you were going to use this pattern for classroom writing, you could introduce it as a game with timed clapping instead of a ball. You would probably also want to change the word *husband* to *brother, sister,* or *friend.* After a round or two of game playing, you could suggest turning the game into a writing activity with each child working with only one letter. Children could use their own names, friends' and family members' names, or other names they are familiar with—even yours. Their finished writings could be bound together as an alphabet book. With any class of young children—but especially one with ELLs—it would be a good idea to brainstorm places and items ahead of time and write several unfamiliar or unphonetic words on the board.

As is, this pattern does not allow much originality, but what if you suggested some changes? Instead of keeping strictly to the rule of one letter sound per verse, writers could describe their own activities with whatever beginning letter fit them. For instance:

T, my name is Terri
And my mother's name is Lisa
We go the supermarket
And buy our food

Here are examples of pieces written by two fourth grade ELLs following this pattern:

L, my name is Lupita
And my friend's name is Brenda
We go to recess and play tetherball

A my name is Antonio
And my friend's name is Joshua.
We go to the soccer field and make goals

Children's writings in this pattern could also be made into a class book that might be more appealing than the alphabet book suggested above because it would reflect students' own lives.

Name Anagrams

Another type of alphabetical pattern children can create is an anagram of their own names. Although the example I offer below would be best for primary-grade children, older students could elaborate upon it by writing longer and more varied sentences. Accomplished writers might wish to turn the basic idea into a complete essay, although in so doing they would lose the anagram format.

> **A**lissa is my name.
> **L**ilies are my favorite flower.
> **I**ce cream is my favorite treat.
> **S**pring is my favorite season.
> **S**aturday is my favorite day.
> **A**ctually, green is my favorite color.

Another pattern of this type uses a child's name followed by a list of things that all start with the same first letter. Such a list can consist of children's characteristics, things they like, or things they can do. Here is one example written by a fourth-grade girl:

> BECCA is so talented she can
> > bake sugar cookies,
> > baby-sit her brother,
> > buy food at the supermarket,
> > build a birdhouse, and
> > bathe the dog.

SEQUENCE PATTERNS

Sequences of letters, numbers, days, and seasons are also patterns that children can follow in their writing. Look for examples of other sequence patterns in traditional nursery rhymes, such as "One, Two, Buckle My Shoe" and "Solomon Gundy," but don't overlook those in many modern children's books, cleverly manipulated by today's authors. Here is one second grader's "days of the week" piece. Although the sentence structure he used is very simple, he produced a clever and entertaining poem.

On the first day of the week
I found a black cat
And it followed me home.

On the second day of the week
I found a red fox
And it followed me home.

On the third day of the week
I found a brown dog
And it followed me home.

On the fourth day of the week
I found a gray squirrel
And it followed me home.

On the fifth day of the week
I found a white rabbit
And it followed me home.

On the sixth day of the week
I found a bluebird
And it followed me home.

On the seventh day of the week
My mother said
Please, no more pets!

AN OFFBEAT PATTERN

For primary-grade children, I especially like the humorous, offbeat patterning in the book, *Q Is for Duck: An Alphabet Guessing Game* by Mary Elting. In it, the letters of the alphabet are used unconventionally to create humor and stimulate children's problem-solving skills.

The title page, for example, reads, "Q is for Duck. Why?" The answer on the following page reads, "Because a duck goes Quack." Later on a "whale" is matched with "e" because a whale is "enormous." As you can see, creating new parts of the pattern is easy for any child who knows something about animals and the sounds of letters. This pattern can also be used to help students build their vocabulary and extend their knowledge about animals. Here are two examples that are not from the book:

W is for penguins. Why?
Because penguins keep their eggs warm.

S is for okapis. Why?
Because okapis have stripes.

This pattern also lends itself to topics other than animals, some of them quite sophisticated. Almost any topic can be developed into a whole book, either by a single child or a class. Here are some examples that could easily be extended:

A is for Carrie. Why?
Because Carrie is athletic.

MV is for George Washington. Why?
Because his home was named Mount Vernon.

D is for oak trees. Why?
Because oak trees are deciduous.

F and S are for a rhombus. Why?
Because a rhombus has four sides.

REPEATED INCIDENT PATTERN

I want to add one more repetitive pattern at this point because it is easy enough for ELL newcomers and strugglers in intermediate grades, yet is not childish. Its repetition also makes it a good learning support. The lines supplied by the pattern are in Italics, so you can see what parts the child wrote.

Go brush your teeth

And make your bed

My mother says to me.

I brush my teeth

And make my bed

And go to let her see.

Go brush your teeth

And make your bed

She says again to me.

I brush my teeth

And make my bed

But this is killing me.

Other children have written the following lines for this pattern:

Go feed the dog . . . And comb your hair

Go wash your face . . . And do your homework

Go turn off the TV . . . And shut off the light

INCREMENTAL PATTERNS

All the patterns I have shown you so far are repeating patterns. Although the words change each time, the structure of the statements or the verses remains the same. But there are other formats called *incremental patterns* that add on new words or phrases with each repetition. "The Twelve Days of Christmas" is an incremental pattern, as is "There's a Hole in the Bottom of the Sea," "The House That Jack Built," and "There Was an Old Woman Who Swallowed a Fly." Although incremental stories and poems tend to be long, they are easy to write because the basic phrases or sentences are used over and over again. They are also good supports for ELLs because the multiple repetitions help them remember new words and spellings. To give an example of an incremental poem, I will quote the first three verses of one written by a first grader. It is not hard to imagine the rest of it.

I had a cat and the cat pleased me.

I fed my cat by yonder tree.

Cat goes fiddle-i-tee.

I had a fish and the fish pleased me.

I fed my fish by yonder tree.

Fish goes glug, glug.

Cat goes fiddle-i-tee.

I had a snake and the snake pleased me.

I fed my snake by yonder tree.

Snakes goes, hiss, hiss.

Fish goes, glug, glug.

Cat goes fiddle-i-tee.

FRAME PATTERNS

All the patterns I've discussed so far can be varied with a single word, short phrase, or the addition of a new line. But there are also "frame" patterns that leave more leeway for variations. One type of frame presents a stem in the first line (or the first two lines) that is repeated in the last line. In between, the lines are mostly open to the writer's ingenuity. The only requirement for these middle lines is uniform length. Because the pattern has a lot of structural repetition, most ELLs and strugglers can reproduce it easily. Here are some frames your students can use.

First line: I am not as big as a (name of an animal, person, or thing)
Second line: A (name of an animal) is bigger than I am.
(Several lines repeating pattern of second line)
Last line: A (very large animal, person or thing) is the biggest thing I know.

First line: A (animal) is a good pet because . . .
(Several lines giving different reasons)
Last line: So why can't I have a (animal)?

First line: I used to think (something) was true . . .
Second line: But now I know (something else) is true.
(Repeat both lines with other things several times.)

First line: I like (something).
Second line: Ask me why . . .

Third line: Because it (give reason).

(Repeat previous line several times with other reasons)

Next line: Because I like (something).

Last line: That's why.

Using the frame just offered, three third-grade girls composed the following patterned piece:

I love candy.
Ask me why.
    Because it comes in many flavors.
    Because it is sweet.
    Because I get it for Halloween.
    Because Mom says it is bad for my teeth.
    Because I don't get much.
Because
Because
Because I love candy.
That's why.

A SOURCE FOR POETRY

One great source I have seen teachers use to stimulate students to try poetry is *A House Is a House for Me* by Mary Ann Hoberman. In the book the repeated pattern, "A house is a house for me," is used in different poetic structures. Following is an example of a poem written in the book's pattern; it doesn't rhyme, but it is so rhythmic that it feels as if it does. The poem was written by Jaime, a fourth-grade ELL.

A math room is a house for nerds, for nerds.
A pen is a house for ink.
A hose is a home for water.
And a house is a house for me.

I want to close this chapter with a patterned poem written by a fourth-grade English-speaking girl. This poem, "Seven Little Monsters," works, I think, because the words that end each stanza's first line have many possible rhyming words. It doesn't matter that some of the ones the writer chose are silly because this kind of poem doesn't make a lot of sense anyway. By including this poem I'm not suggesting anything new; I just like the rollicking rhythm and the original illustrations that go with each stanza.

MORE PATTERNS AHEAD

Although my suggestions for using patterns to support children's writing stop here for now, don't think that you've seen the last of them. I will discuss more complex forms of patterned writing in future chapters, when we look at the uses of popular culture, the plot and style patterns in imaginative writing, and the creation of original poetry. Because patterns of different types are a significant element of literary writing, students should learn to be on the lookout for them as they read and to use them in their own writing.

SEVEN LITTLE MONSTERS

Seven monsters in a row,
See the seven monsters go.

Monster one is in a tree.

And monster two is chasing me.

Monster three is gobbling up my door.

Monster four is resting on the floor.

Number five is eating a dame.

Monster six is playing a game.

Number seven is amazingly slow.

Seven monsters in a row.

Making trouble, there they go!

Pattern poem by a fourth-grade girl

CHAPTER 3

Short Messages

Although we don't usually consider messages that consist of only a phrase or a couple of sentences to be school writing activities, these messages are everywhere in the world outside the classroom, and many people make their living producing them. Most short messages do their job of warning, announcing, reminding, or informing people, very well. Even single-word messages, such as "Push" and "Stop" are valuable to have around.

BENEFITS OF SHORT MESSAGES

I don't think I have to persuade you that children will enjoy writing short, meaningful messages and that they will feel very grown up doing so. But I do have to point out that there are special benefits for ELLs and struggling writers. First, being asked to write a phrase or a sentence or two will not intimidate them the way the prospect of a long story or a science report might. Second, even children who are strangers to literary and academic writing are quite familiar with the short messages they see on banners, cereal boxes, street signs, and T-shirts; thus they already have much of the context they need to write their own. Finally, short messages provide opportunities for building vocabulary, practicing spelling, and constructing sentences just as effectively as long pieces of writing do. The only writing skills missing from short messages are the more sophisticated processes of idea development and sentence coordination, and those can be learned in doing the other types of writing covered in this book.

DIFFERENT KINDS OF SHORT MESSAGES

To begin the discussion of teaching short-message writing, let's survey the territory. Below are several different kinds of short, simple messages that children can write. All of them fit into the regular doings of elementary-level classrooms.

- ❖ Signs
- ❖ Labels
- ❖ Slogans
- ❖ Titles
- ❖ Warnings
- ❖ Sayings
- ❖ Nicknames and pseudonyms
- ❖ Reminders
- ❖ Dos and don'ts
- ❖ Captions for pictures

As early as kindergarten, children fall easily into the habit of making labels and signs and writing words to accompany their drawings. One classroom opportunity that comes to mind is the need for labels marking supply shelves, work areas, and children's places and possessions. Classrooms also need signs to remind children what to do or not do, such as, "Wash your hands" and "Walk quietly in the hall." If teachers would hold off on labeling and decorating classrooms so completely before the beginning of the school year, children would be better able to see the needs and volunteer to help make their classroom a functional and attractive place. Below is a sign from a grade 1–2 mixed-language classroom reminding children about safety.

A safety poster by a first grader

CURRICULAR LABELS, SIGNS, AND SLOGANS

There are also curriculum-related opportunities for labels, signs, and drawings all year long. Many teachers organize their classes into cooperative learning groups, seated together, and have children name their groups. Often teachers post the group names on signs dangling over children's desks, on charts recording completed assignments, and above displays of group work. Having children write the signs instead of the teacher is a good beginning, but the basic idea can also be carried further into slogans, group member nicknames or pseudonyms, and more. The creation of these short messages can be repeated many times over the course of the school year, as groups are reconstituted or new units studied. Think about the following two possible contexts.

An intermediate-grade class studying the solar system could be divided into groups according to the planet each is concentrating on. Two groups might be named "The Mars Stars" and "The Jumping Jupiters." Planet groups could create slogans in addition to their names, such as "Venus Rocks" (a pun on the fact that Venus is a rock-based planet) or "Earth Kids Are in Orbit." Group members could also invent nicknames for themselves related to the characteristics of their planet, such as "Many Moons Marco" (member of the Saturn group) and put their nicknames on buttons or T-shirts to wear. To carry the idea further, a group could produce a large poster of its planet with a title and brief explanations of its most prominent features. The whole class could also make a set of planet fact cards for a game called "Name the Planet" or to accompany oral presentations on planet research.

BUILDING COMMUNITY

In primary-level classrooms, teachers often spend a lot of time creating a sense of community among their students. Part of that endeavor could consist of creating labels, signs, and drawings to reinforce caring behavior and recognition of others' rights. After a discussion of the signs children think they need or want, the teacher could use photos of common neighborhood signs as supportive models for writing. For example, "Caution: Men Working" could be the basis for a sign that says "Caution: Children Working." "Slow Down: School Zone" could be transformed into "Quiet Down: Reading Zone." "Beware of the Dog" could become "Beware of Wet Paintings." In addition to warning signs, children could create signs with street names for their row or group of desks. And each individual desk could have a mailbox sign with the street number and name of the child living there. Children could also name their community and post its name and slogan on the classroom door, like this: "Gluetown. Population: 25. We Stick Together."

At the same time, community-building includes slogans about caring behavior that can be expressed on posters. "To have friends, be a friend," "Teasing hurts," and "Taking without asking isn't fair," are examples of slogans that occur to my adult mind, but I think that children could do better by stating their feelings in their own words and pictures.

Stems for Community-Building

Another kind of short message that aids community-building is one that uses a stem the teacher has supplied, followed by children's phrases or single words. This kind of message is very practical in primary classrooms because children can write about their interests, class behavior, subject matter, or an event outside of school, and they can work in small groups or individually without further help from the teacher. These stems are not meant to initiate full writings, but to begin a list of short statements about how children should act under certain circumstances. Here are some possible stems:

> When the teacher is busy, we . . .
> When someone is talking, I . . .
> When I finish my work, I can . . .
> On the playground, I should . . .
> If I don't have the supplies I need, I can . . .

Creative Thinking Stems

Stems can also be used to stimulate children's thinking about personal needs and interests:

> If I had a pet, I would . . .
> If I wanted a new friend, I would . . .
> If I were grown up, I could . . .

Here is one example of a second grader's stem writing about what she'd do if she were boss of the school. It, and others written by her classmates, grew out of a discussion about school rules and the job of the principal.

> If I were the boss of our school, I'd make these rules.
> ❖ No throwing school supplies because they could hurt somebody.

- ❖ Be very quiet or else you'll get in trouble.
- ❖ Don't run in the halls.
- ❖ Let everyone play in playground games.

BOOK CELEBRATION MESSAGES

Another way that children can write short messages is by celebrating books they've read. Although teachers do not ordinarily expect primary-level children to do book reports, this activity serves the same purposes in a simpler way. On a cutout of a book cover, a child can draw a scene that represents the book she's read and write the title of the book and the names of the author and illustrator. The cutout can then be pasted on a larger sheet where the child writes one or two short comments about the book. Within the capabilities of young writers, their comments should convey the message, "I liked this book, and this is what it's about."

ACADEMIC MESSAGES

Children too young to write out science or social studies reports can do academic writing by making labels and captions for pictures. At right is an example of one done by a child in a mixed-language classroom.

A labeled picture for science by Alissa

MESSAGES FOR OLDER STUDENTS

All the short messages I've described so far are simple ones because I've been thinking about primary-level children and the limited skills of newcomer ELLs and struggling writers. But there are certainly more demanding contexts in which experienced ELLs and their older classmates could write short messages. Again, I will resort to a list outlining the territory because I can't describe all of the possibilities.

- ❖ Definitions
- ❖ Headlines
- ❖ Lessons or main ideas from stories
- ❖ Explanations

All of these short messages demand high-level thinking and good reading skills. Writing out the moral of a story or a headline for a news article means that students need to understand the whole text and be able to boil it down to its essential meaning. In any classroom, this is probably best done in a partnership arrangement, at least for early attempts. On the other hand, most students can write definitions alone if they have already become familiar with the words and their meanings from classwork.

Definitions

When it comes to understanding the meanings of new words in books or content areas, teachers tend to give students definitions to copy or have them look up the words in a dictionary. Neither way helps students much because the definitions are usually just as hard to understand as the original words. Teaching vocabulary is far more effective for ELLs and native English speakers when the students do the following: write down what they think words mean when they first encounter them; test their definitions against those others have written; refine their definitions after discussion and reading. It might also be good to have students revisit their definitions at a later time, say after a unit has been finished, to see how their understandings of words may have changed.

Below are just a few definitions that intermediate-level students wrote after studying content units. They are not the ones originally written by individual students, but those that the class agreed on after they had finished the units. Although these definitions may not mesh with our adult sense of the words' meanings, they work for the students who are using them.

- ❖ **Exploration**—Going someplace where nobody has been and studying it so that other people can go there, too.
- ❖ **Pilgrims**—People who came to America from England in 1620 to have freedom.
- ❖ **Gravity**—The physical power that pulls people and things to the earth.
- ❖ **Angle**—The space between two straight lines that come together at one end.

Story Morals and Lessons

Being able to write the moral or lesson of a story grows out of long experience in reading stories and poems where there is an overall life lesson to ponder. In the beginning, teachers can read stories aloud and draw tentative ideas out from children. Fairy tales like "The Little Red Hen" have one clear lesson; others, such as "Cinderella," offer more open-ended possibilities. Many young children's books also contain lessons that children can sympathize with, if not completely comprehend. Think about *Leo the Late Bloomer*, *The Giving Tree*, *The Paper Bag Princess*, and *I'll Love You Forever*.

In discussing a book, children's ideas about morals and lessons may be way off base much of the time. You should accept their ideas but not hesitate to offer your own interpretation and ask children to consider it. Because children are children, there is no magic trick to bring them to the heart of a story. They will take each story personally or reject it as not being relevant to their world. Still, some stories are so transparent that their lessons are impossible to miss. The most well-known stories with lessons are *Aesop's Fables*, Joel Chandler Harris's tales of Br'er Rabbit, and Rudyard Kipling's *Just So Stories*. You can use any or all of these to help students get the idea of stories teaching lessons to readers.

Purposes and Main Ideas

When children begin to read stories of their own choosing, teachers have to be more cautious about asking to identify lessons. We need to recognize that many stories are written as pure entertainment and make children aware of that fact. As your students progress as readers, it would be better to change the question from "What is the lesson?" to "What is the purpose or main idea of this story?"

By third grade, most students should be able to find a main idea or a purpose in a story and articulate it in writing. Still, it helps to give them a simple frame to use—for example:

I think the main idea of the story (title) is _____.
I think the story (title) doesn't have any main idea. Its purpose is to _____.

The teacher should demonstrate how to choose one of the frames and complete it.

Newspaper Headlines

Strange as it may seem, studying newspaper headlines is a logical outgrowth of identifying main ideas. The purpose of a headline is to give readers a short message about the story's content, so they can decide whether or not they want to read it. I'm suggesting that teachers use this activity with intermediate students because it will help them to get to the central meaning of nonfiction pieces and write succinctly. It also initiates them into the habit of reading newspapers, something they might not do otherwise.

In teaching this activity, you can use short articles from regular newspapers or newspapers written expressly for children. They should begin by introducing one article of interest to students every few days during current events time, following it with a brief discussion of its content and the fit of its headline. After gaining some understanding of newspaper stories and their headlines, students may be ready to write headlines of their own for existing articles. You should present one article, without its headline to the whole class and let everyone try their hand at writing one. Afterward, students can compare their headlines and decide which ones they like best. The trick to writing a good headline is being able to combine accuracy and clarity with brevity, so you might limit the number of words students are allowed to use in their headlines after they have some experience writing them.

In suggesting that students write definitions, morals, main ideas, and headlines in the form of short messages, I have a dual purpose. On the surface these writings are quick and easy ways for children to communicate something meaningful, but at a deeper level they are important thinking activities that will help children learn how to find meaning in everything they read. They lay the foundation for every act of comprehension and every demonstration of comprehension students will asked to perform in all the years of schooling to come.

Explanations

Giving and receiving explanations is another activity that increases students' comprehension. As a classroom teacher, you have probably noticed that you understand math operations and scientific processes better after you have explained them to your students. A good way to approach the teaching of explanations is to give them regularly. Your students deserve to know why you chose to give a particularly complicated assignment and how you expect them to work through it. In turn, you have a right to know why students misbehave or neglect their work. What I am suggesting is that oral and written explanations should be a part of the classroom routine. In the case of missing homework, for example, I think it is reasonable to expect that a student who didn't turn it in will write a short message explaining what went wrong for him. In some classrooms the teacher may have to supply students with a model or a framework for explanations. In others, students will intuitively know how to explain themselves.

During the daily writing time you can suggest that students occasionally write a few sentences of explanation about their habits or personal preferences, such as how they choose books to read for pleasure or why they like certain sports. These personal explanations are not for general sharing. They are a way for students to better understand their own behavior. On the other hand, students can occasionally write explanations they intend to give to another person as part of a note of apology. One first-grade teacher I know has children write notes to their parents when they misbehave, telling them what "poor choice" they made and what "better choice" they will make next time.

Incidental Writing

As I suggested earlier, a lot of short message writing grows out of class meetings and incidental classroom happenings. The example below is from a classroom poster developed by a grades 4–5 class after their teacher scolded them about saying "I'm bored'" so often. Halfway into her stern lecture, this teacher realized that she wasn't getting through to her students and turned to humor instead. After a lot of silly interaction, this is what the class produced.

> Bored? Try Our Remedies.
> ❖ Flood your sister's room.
> ❖ Chase your dog's tail.
> ❖ Straighten uncooked macaroni.
> ❖ Collect clouds in a box.
> ❖ Look for your brain.
> ❖ Drink milk with a fork.
> ❖ Blow back at the wind.
> ❖ Fill the Grand Canyon with spit.
> ❖ Teach paper clips to dance.
> ❖ Make paper back into wood.
> ❖ Drown your baseball cards.
> ❖ Talk yourself to death.

Miscellaneous Messages

I've saved some other student examples of short public messages for the end of this chapter because they don't fit into the contexts I've talked about. I guess you'd call them "miscellaneous." Although the contexts of these messages are not described, I think you can figure them out and imagine others that would also stimulate writing.

Messages on Classroom and Hallway Posters

Recycle Your Used Notebook Paper Here.

Help Celebrate Martin Luther King's Birthday
Party in the Gym
Tues, Jan 21
3:30 PM
Admission 50 cents

Keep to the right in the halls.

Exaggeration for Fun

❖ Our car is so old that it is insured for fire, train collisions, and buffalo stampedes.
❖ The man was so tall he was chopped down for a tree by mistake.
❖ The apple was so small, the worm used it as an appetizer.
❖ My dad was so mad that the steam from his ears cooked our dinner.
❖ The test was so easy that my brain took off and went to bed.

Humorous Definitions

❖ A desk is a dungeon with a dragon in it that eats all my homework.
❖ A teacher is someone who knows almost everything. But when it comes to cars, she flunks!
❖ A hockey stick is something you can always burn if you get mad at it.
❖ A dictionary has all the words that you're not looking for.

Text and captions about animals

Mixed-Media Messages

These are messages expressed equally in words and pictures. The display above, in a primary level mixed-language classroom, pairs labeled drawings of animals with short written texts.

Here is one (at right) illustrating and explaining pond life as part of a science unit.

POSSIBILITIES

What you haven't seen much of in this chapter is academic writing. That topic and its examples more properly belong in Chapter 8, which focuses on a variety of longer pieces of content-area writing. Still, I hope my descriptions of the pos-

Captions and labels explaining pond life

sibilities for writing short messages will move you to think more about how you can incorporate them into units and lessons where your main emphasis is on learning content and skills. Short messages, whether private or public, are an important means for ELLs and novice writers to express their knowledge, ideas, and feelings.

CHAPTER 4

Personal Writing

Up until now I have been suggesting activities that grow out of the process of building a context for writing that I described in Chapter 1. But personal writing brings some new dimensions into the mix. In principle and practice, personal writing is different from the kinds of writing described in Chapters 2 and 3 because most of the time it is private, individual, and instrumental. I say "private" because personal writing is intended for one or more specific people, and sometimes only for the writer himself. Personal writing is "individual" because it relates only to the interests of the writer and the recipient. And it is "instrumental" because the writing is not an end product; it is meant to serve some other purpose. Let me illustrate with a simple example. When I write to a friend about meeting for lunch on Thursday, that message is not shared with other people; it concerns matters that only she and I care about, and the sole purpose of the note is to facilitate our meeting. It has no artistic or cultural value.

Because of these characteristics, personal writing in the classroom requires some changes in procedures. Teachers can't provide a background context for notes children want to write to their friends or for journal entries. They can't set a certain day for writing personal requests or for complaining about personal slights. They can't even supply supportive models for most kinds of personal writing. What's more, teachers should not grade personal writings or even read most pieces because they weren't meant for them.

RATIONALE FOR TEACHING

If these things are true, then why are we talking about teaching personal writing? Because children need help to achieve clarity, focus, and completeness in the kinds of writing they will be doing regularly for the rest of their lives. It seems to me that this is reason enough to focus on personal writing in the classroom.

But how do we get around the nonintervention principles of personal writing I have just mentioned? If teachers should keep their hands off personal writing most of the time, how can they teach it or help children practice it? Well, fortunately, there are some ways, but you may have to change how things work in your classroom. You can, for example, provide time in the school day for students to write notes, reflections, and reminders; write personal notes or e-mails to students about their work or behavior and encourage them to respond; ask students to keep journals (or, if you have enough classroom computers, to write blogs); set up a classroom or school-wide post office system; arrange for pen pals from another class or another school; encourage students to add comments to their parents in the regular classroom newsletter; encourage students to write to friends or family about field trips, school events, or school projects; invite students to write comments to you about lessons you've taught (if you can bear the criticism!); or start your own computer wiki and urge students to join in. (A wiki is an interactive blog. One person starts it and others respond, and ideas flow more freely.)

To facilitate any of these writing opportunities you need to establish some long-term protocols, ideally at the beginning of the school year. Personal writing does not belong to a single unit of study or to a passing student interest. You are going to have to rely on the provision of time, instruction, and willing student involvement. If you think this sounds a lot like writing workshop, you're right. The only differences are that you're not focusing on writing as an end in itself, and you're not including conferencing, revision, or editing in the process.

TIME PROVISION

I've noticed that most teachers who use writing workshop or journal writing in their classrooms set a time early in the day, presumably because that's when students are fresh. But if I were going to set a time for personal writing, I would have it just before students go home, when they would be most inclined to reflect on the day just passed and to write reminders to themselves, notes to their parents, or invitations to their friends.

Although the amount of time you set aside may vary with the age and skills of your students, I think 20 minutes is about the limit for any age group. In addition, you might include a couple of short writing breaks—say, five minutes—spaced throughout the day. One good time might be after a long or difficult lesson, so students could comment to you about it. Another good time might be just after the lunch recess, when they are likely to have something to brag or complain about. If a student feels that there is nothing she wants to write about at a particular time or on a particular day, she ought to be able to read, do puzzles, or clean out her desk instead. I'd worry only if a child was opting out of writing on a regular basis.

In addition to time, children need instruction. For common writing problems and technical matters, you can use mini-lessons; for introducing different kinds of writing, you can use models and simulations; and for motivation, you can set up activities that provide purpose and opportunity for interaction with other writers.

MINI-LESSONS

Mini-lessons are most appropriate for dealing with special occasions or specific writing problems. What I mean by occasions are the events that call for some sort of personal writing, such as an upcoming field trip, the arrival of a set of pen-pal letters, or the emergence of a question that no one in the class can answer. Special occasions are easy to deal with because the need for action is clear and the same guidance is appropriate for all students. You can give a mini-lesson on including correct and complete information in notes to parents about the upcoming field trip or properly addressing pen-pal letters.

Specific writing problems are trickier because they vary among students, and some students may not have any problems at a given time. You should call together only the students who are in need of help now for this mini-lesson. You may wonder how you'll know who is having which writing problems if you're not monitoring students' personal writing. This is a legitimate question, but there is also a legitimate answer: You'll know because you regularly write to children and they regularly respond to you, and because most of their problems are also readily apparent in their regular class work.

One type of error children frequently make is using the wrong pronoun. You may wish you had a dollar for every time you've heard or read, "Me and him went down to the mall." Several of the teachers I know are always ready for this kind of error with a couple of mini-lessons shaped around practical arguments that students understand better than formal grammar rules. You might say, "Does 'Me ate eggs for breakfast' sound right to you? Does 'Her is wearing a blue sweater' sound right?" By third grade these sentences sound wrong to most children. But if students seem unsure, you can pull out an overhead with sentences taken from a couple of the fiction books students have been reading that illustrate proper pronouns use and ask students to read them aloud. During the ensuing discussion, the remedy that emerges is for students to test pronouns by using them singly to see how they sound. You can end the lesson by asking students to create their own sentences using the models on the overhead.

When dealing with personal writing, however, mini-lessons are more often about clarity than grammar or mechanics. After all, most recipients of personal writing are pretty tolerant of a few misspelled words and missing commas. But when messages aren't clear, there can be big trouble. You can explain that if children are giving directions to their house or to the site of today's soccer game, the receiver must be able to follow those directions to the right place. If they are recommending a book to a friend, writing the title and author's name correctly is important. If they want Mom and Dad to give them an iPhone for their birthday, they have to be clear about the color and the special features you prefer. It also helps if they can tell them where to buy it.

USING MODELS

Showing and explaining examples of different types of personal writing are also a part of instruction. You want your students to examine the form and style of typical friendly letters, quick informational notes, and personal reminders to see how they work. You can model through your own correspondence with adults or children. Without getting into a deep analysis, you can point out how you and other writers got their points across briefly, clearly, and completely and how you adjusted your style and tone for the person to whom you were writing. Here is an example of a personal note written by a second-grade boy about a school field trip.

> Dear Matt,
> On the bus Ryan and I read a book called "Big Machines at Work." We read until we got tired. When we got to the Geology Museum we saw glowing rocks. I got to pick out a rock to take home. The rocks had gold in them. Then we went to Babcock Hall to eat ice cream. I had Cherry Almond. We got on the bus again. It took us to Madison General Hospital where we got on another bus. Then we went back to school. It was a good field trip.
>
> Your friend,
> Eric

And here are two notes from third-grade ELLs to their teacher. This teacher writes to her students regularly and expects them to write back to her.

Dear Miss Lindley,

My sisters are gone and I miss them. Do you want to no there age? One of them is two and the other sister is three They have been gone for a long time but I can't white (wait) for my sisters to come back. They are coming in December. Wait in tell I tell you the best part is you are a grate teacher You are just the best.

    Think you for being the best teacher in the world.

Think you
Alexis

Dear Miss Lindley

My granma is coming on Saturday in the morning I don't know what time she is going to come. She lives in Mexico. She's going to california with my aunt. Then my aunt is going to bring her coputer so I culd yous it and play games in it.

Christian

SIMULATIONS

At times, teachers use simulations in instruction because real situations don't always come up when you need them. Simulations are imaginative writings that parallel the forms and purposes of real writing. One teacher I know introduced "excuse" writing to her third graders by having them assume the role of a student or a parent writing to her about missing homework. Although the situation was not real at the time for any of the students, they took to it eagerly because most of them had had that experience in the past. Below is one of these letters.

Dear Mrs. Bohlman,

Please excuse my daughter, Julie, for not handing in her homework. You see my husband is a wizard and left his lab open by mistake. My two-year-old son, Jimmy, got in and took my husband's Disappearing Powder and sprinkled it all over Julie's homework. So now who knows where it is?

Sorry!

Mrs. D

Another teacher used a simulation to get her students to produce written complaints not based on reality. She asked them to imagine that they were their own desks and what those desks would say to them if they could write notes of complaint. Amazingly, the tone and content of the complaints students wrote were very realistic. Here is what one fourth grader wrote:

> Dear Glenn,
>
> You always drop my jaw and you never clean my mouth! Sometimes you write on my head. I'm always getting moved out of position and I'm stuffed. You always kick my feet and you put your elbows on my face. I'm getting tired of you slamming your chair into me, and besides, how do you think it feels? It hurts, right chair? Yeah. How would you feel if a pencil dropped on your head every ten seconds? I hate it! Why do you stick your hand in my mouth? Next time I'll bite your hand!
>
> Your Desk

MOTIVATING PERSONAL WRITING

Students are moved to do personal writing by their intrinsic need to communicate and by the efforts of others to communicate with them. Unfortunately, this need doesn't materialize spontaneously in most classrooms. Not only are classrooms physically well insulated from the world outside, tradition has built a philosophical wall between the business of school and the lives of children, causing teachers to believe that they must assign writing rather than allow it to emerge from children's needs and interests. Worse still, the overemphasis on testing and test preparation in recent years has left many teachers feeling that they cannot spare any time or effort for things that will not be tested. Nevertheless, I hope I can persuade you that welcoming real communication into your classroom will advance, not impede, your students' writing progress.

To illustrate the ways in which teachers can open the door to children's intrinsic motivation, I offer three vignettes. The situations described are composites of what I have seen in various classrooms and what teachers have told me in interviews. The teachers named in the vignettes are not real people.

CONTRIBUTING TO THE CLASSROOM NEWSLETTER

In her second-grade classroom Helen Kapner sends home a weekly newsletter to let parents know what the class has been working on and how well they are doing. At the beginning of the year, she wrote a draft of each newsletter and projected it on a screen for the class to add to and correct. Although she made no intentional errors in her draft, she sometimes forgot to include things that the children thought were important. After reading the draft aloud, children were encouraged to make comments and offer suggestions. Ms. Kapner accepted the consensus of the class and made the appropriate changes and additions. The next day, she handed out printed copies of the finished newsletter for the children to take home.

As the year has worn on, Ms. Kapner has added a new twist to the process. Now she puts spaces in the newsletter for children to add personal messages to their parents. Since she's writing about classwork in general, she encourages the children to write about their specific involvement in or reactions to the work the class has done.

Although Ms. Kapner does not ask to see what the children write, many show her their messages. She sees that most often they cite particular lessons or class happenings they enjoy, and only occasionally mention what they don't like or don't do well. She also notices that children tend to adopt her spelling and sentence structure in their own messages. They even start their notes with "Dear Parents," as she does. It seems clear to the teacher that children are picking up on the basics of this kind of writing and using them in their own messages.

TEACHER-STUDENT CORRESPONDENCE

Richard Davis, a fifth-grade teacher, keeps up a regular e-mail correspondence with his students. He doesn't write to all of them every day, but tries to get a note out to each of his 28 students once a week. That's five or six notes a day, but he manages by keeping notes brief. Although he does not tell students that they must write back to him, he encourages them to do so and prods those who are silent too long. "I need to hear from you personally," he says to the class and to individuals. "I want to know if you like what we're doing in class and if you're having any problems. I also want to know how things are going for you when I'm not around, say in the lunch room or on the playground." As a greater spur to action, Mr. Davis gives more pointed messages from time to time. He might say, "I'm thinking that I might be moving too fast in our science unit. After all, this stuff is really hard. How do you feel about it?" or "You kids are usually so good about getting your homework in on time, but today there were several papers missing. Write and tell me what was going on with you."

SCHOOL POST OFFICE

For several years teacher Lillian Alden has run a school-wide post office out of her sixth-grade classroom. What started out very simply as an intermittent two-classroom exchange of letters between students has developed into a weekly delivery and a daily sorting system. Ms. Alden's students also sell stamps and envelopes twice a week through the school store for five cents apiece. At first they were hesitant to charge for stamps, but they soon found out that other students wanted the stamps they had designed and produced even if they weren't going to use them on letters.

Two students act as sorters, daily taking the letters that have been deposited in a box outside their classroom and putting them into a set of cubbyholes resting on a large table at the back of their classroom. If a letter doesn't have a legible classroom address, it is sent back to the return address; if it doesn't have a return address, it goes into the dead letter box, which is also outside in the hall.

Once a week, the sorters take the mail out of the cubbyholes and put room number labels on each package of letters and a rubber band around it. They also arrange packages according to classroom location. Since there are usually no more than five letters a day, this process takes only a few minutes.

After the sorting, three mail carriers deliver mail to classrooms in each of the three hallways of the school by putting each package on a teacher's desk. Any errors in addresses have to be handled by classroom teachers.

Although the flow of mail ebbs from time to time, the teachers in this school work to keep it going. As a group they decided long ago that having their students write personal letters to their friends in other classrooms was a worthwhile activity, so they actively promote it and offer their students various small inducements for writing, such as no-homework days.

One unexpected benefit has come to Ms. Alden's class in the form of complaints from students in other classrooms. They enjoy discussing the complaints together and having one of their groups answer them. Sometimes they wish out loud that there were more complaints.

GIVING FEEDBACK

Along with time, instruction, and practice, feedback helps children improve their personal writing. In my experience, students normally get feedback only from their teacher, and that feedback focuses on correctness rather than the effectiveness of a message.

Increasing feedback to students is difficult. In the course of everyday life, the people we write to do not let us know how well we have communicated. Yet because personal writing is instrumental, it is important for children to find out whether their writings did the job they were intended to do, so some pump priming by the teacher is necessary. You might ask parents to discuss their children's notes with them, pointing out what was clear and not clear, what additional information they would have liked, and how the notes made them feel. Some parents will carry through on this assignment; others, for various reasons, will not. If, however, students regularly exchange messages through a school or classroom mail system, teachers have more control over feedback. They can remind their students to let their correspondents know about the effectiveness of their messages and ask their colleagues to do the same. They can even make giving feedback a special assignment from time to time.

Actually, the most meaningful feedback cannot be planned; it just happens. If parents don't give permission for their daughter to go on a field trip because she didn't make it clear that they had to, she will think about that as she remains at school while her classmates are on their trip. If friends all bring a food contribution to one student's cookout, as he wanted them to, then he can bask in the success of his communication. When personal writing is practiced regularly in the classroom, both success and failure in communicating will occur and make a lasting impression on young writers.

A Personal Note

Dear Readers,

After finishing this chapter I had some qualms about including it with the rest. Although I am convinced there is value in having personal letter writing in school, I am not sure that all of you will agree. I realize that there are two big factors working against this practice: the inherent lack of teacher supervision and the outside pressures for teaching only the things that are tested. But if you take the bold steps of making time, creating opportunities, and giving some instruction, I think you will see the results in improved writing in regular classroom work and in greater student enthusiasm for writing in general. I hope that you'll give it a try—and you can always write letters of complaint to me if you're displeased.

Sincerely,

Joanne

CHAPTER 5

Social Communication

Much of the writing ordinary people do is for the purpose of obtaining or preserving a place in society. We write to forge bonds with others, to gain benefits or status, and to fulfill our social obligations. The most common examples of social communications are job inquiries, thank-you notes, invitations, announcements, and letters to strangers. Not only does our society expect us to write these things, it also expects us to follow the conventions set in the past and still followed by most people. That's why I think of this type of writing as "conventional communication" as well as social communication.

CHILDREN'S NEEDS

Children from any cultural background have little experience with social communication apart from the thank-you notes their parents make them write. As parents or as recipients of such notes, you know they are usually brief, vague about what the gift was, and weak in enthusiasm for it. We forgive them because they are just kids and hope they will eventually learn to do things right.

Except for thank-you notes, there are few opportunities for children to learn about social communication outside of school. For this reason alone, we have an obligation to teach them, and the elementary grades are the place to start. At the same time, we must recognize that not all forms of social communication are appropriate for elementary-age children. There is no point in teaching condolence notes or business letters when children have no immediate need for them. Those writings would be just exercises without any sense of purpose, and children would soon forget their conventions.

What teachers should do is to look realistically at the situations elementary students are likely to confront. Then they have to be ready to seize opportunities for social communication when they come up and uncover opportunities in content areas where they are not so obvious.

Below are some of the situations and possibilities I see for social communication in grades K–6:

- ❖ Thank-you notes
- ❖ Invitations to classroom celebrations and performances
- ❖ Letters of request, complaint, and congratulations
- ❖ Public announcements and requests
- ❖ Articles in school newsletters
- ❖ Greeting cards
- ❖ Letters to strangers

I need to point out that ELLs are likely to be especially needy when it comes to social communication in English. Whatever conventions they know are from a different culture. They may be suitable for communicating with other people of that culture but not with native English speakers. I think it would be great, when addressing notes or announcements to parents of ELLs, to follow the conventions of their culture as much as possible. However, that may require seeking help from a knowledgeable adult of the same culture.

THE BASICS OF INSTRUCTION

When a particular form of writing is outside of children's experience, and also bound by conventions, teaching calls for the generous use of models and frameworks. If, for instance, students are going to write to the local school board requesting that the school library be kept open in the evening, they need to see some real letters of request. As they write, they may need a general request framework to fit their words into. In addition, their teacher will have to teach some appropriate conventions directly. Children do not intuitively know that a date is necessary at the top of any social letter and a return address on any business letter.

PROVIDING SUPPORTS

Process supports for social communication come in two different forms: frameworks and guide cards. When a particular type of writing is being done for the first time, a framework is often necessary. It gives students the conventions they are not familiar with, while allowing them to fill the rest of the space with their own ideas and words. The teacher explains that they may also change words in parts of the framework to make it fit the situation. A guide card is a reminder of things students have been taught and already practiced. It is small enough to be placed next to students' papers for reference while writing.

Below are examples of a framework and a guide card for writing a thank-you note to a parent who has helped the class in some way. Both will work equally well for a group thank-you or an individual note as long as the teacher makes clear that individual notes can be less formal than a group letter by showing models of both.

Framework for a Thank-You Note

Date _____

Dear Ms. _____

(I or We) want to thank you for _____

It was really nice of you to _____

(I or We) hope you come to our classroom again soon.

Your friend(s),

Signature(s)

Guide Card for a Thank-You Note

Dear (Mr., Mrs., Miss, Ms., or First name).

Say thank you and mention what the person did for you.

Describe what the person did.

Say something to make the person feel good.

Use an appropriate closing.

Sign your note.

Welcome letters, invitations to special events, and announcements are also frequent forms of social communication. Here is a vignette, describing the process of an actual teacher and her class preparing to have a substitute the following week. That preparation will include writing a letter to the substitute.

Because teacher Mary Starrs will be out of school all next week, she has been talking to her fifth-grade class about how to behave when a substitute teacher is in charge. Today she suggests that each student write a letter to the substitute, making her feel welcome and giving her the necessary information about the class. Although she has no models to show them, they have written social communications before for other purposes, so she reminds them of some of the conventions.

The students immediately warm to the idea of writing to their substitute, even though they had been expecting a different writing activity today. Ms. Starrs begins by asking students to group themselves in teams of four to discuss what they think they should tell a substitute teacher about their classroom and themselves. After a few minutes of lively discussion, she calls the class to order and asks them to tell her how to begin the letter. Several suggestions are supplied, and she writes the ones the class likes best on the board for students to choose from.

When it comes to content, Ms. Starrs also asks for student suggestions. At first, many of them are personal ("I'll tell her I have red hair") or of minor importance ("We've been working on speaking correctly"). Ms. Starrs guides the class back on course by saying, "This could be a long letter. Let's put in it only the things a substitute needs to know." With this prompt, students turn to rules, jobs, and helpful hints for running the classroom. After writing down several of their suggestions in full sentences, Ms. Starrs points out that most of the sentences have the same form. Thus there is no need for her to repeat the sentences; she will write down only the ideas.

After this introduction, Ms. Starrs sends the class back to their tables where they are to discuss again for a few minutes what to put into their letters. When the talking time is up, the students begin writing eagerly. A few of them look to the board occasionally for words or sentence forms, but most are self-sufficient. On each table is a card with "No Excuses Spelling Words" that the students can also refer to. Ms. Starrs moves around the room helping and encouraging those few students who are finding the task rough going.

Following is the first draft of the letter written by one of the students during the class session described. She edited it the following day so it could be put into a folder for the substitute teacher. Although the use of conventions and the welcoming tone in this letter are typical of the ones other students wrote, it focuses on only one kind of information the substitute needs to know. For that reason, other students' letters were also included in the folder.

Dear Ms. Gould,

It is nice to meet you. I would like you to know a few things about the jobs we have in are class. For example, the zoo cepr watrs the stik bugs items. The tabl captens bismis ther grup to line up properly. And the line manitoer tells us wen we can go or lineup betr. Those are a fuw of the jobs and wen you com you will see them all in acshin and you won't be disapoyntid.

Esmeralda

The instructional pattern you have seen in the samples and vignette is essentially the same for any type of social communication. Although I did not put a special emphasis on models in them, please remember that they are an important part of this type of instruction. Most children have not had the opportunity to examine—or even to see—a real example of a social communication before they are expected to write one.

EXAMPLES OF SOCIAL COMMUNICATIONS

I devote the rest of this chapter to examples of different kinds of social communications written by children of different ages and different backgrounds. Those written by ELLs from high-poverty schools in Oregon are accompanied by the students' real first names. On other writings the names are marked with asterisks to let you know they are pseudonyms for native English speakers from my former school in Wisconsin. Not only will these examples serve as models if you decide to teach some forms of social communication, they will also suggest what you need to include on frameworks or guide cards for those forms.

AUTHOR BIOGRAPHY

This blurb was attached to a book of a fifth-grade girl's writings.

Susan Sanders was born and raised in Madison, Wisconsin, and still enjoys the Madison area. She lives with her mother, father, sister, and cat Amanda. Miss Sanders is currently being educated at Crestwood Elementary School and will graduate soon.

Miss Sanders has written several well-known poems and has had many of her pieces put in books. She has published two books, one titled *Tongue Twisters*.

Currently, she is experimenting by writing a fictional book titled *The Inner Sphere*.

Miss Sanders started writing in her youth and has been writing ever since. Besides writing, she enjoys skiing, gymnastics and music and has high hopes to become an architect.

SCHOOL NEWSLETTER ANNOUNCEMENT

This announcement appeared in a fourth-grade class's monthly newsletter.

Glow Stick Sale

We are selling glow sticks. If you pay one dollar you get one glow stick. We are selling glow sticks because we are raising money for field trips. The people who are selling them are anyone from Mrs. Staver's and Mr. Lindberg's class. They are selling them before and after school.

William and Marianna

SCHOOL NEWSLETTER ARTICLE

This short article appeared in the same newsletter as the announcement above.

At Davis elementary School 4th and 5th graders go to strings. They play the violin, viola and cello. They go to strings every other day. The teacher's name is Mrs. Hirsch.

"Playing the violin isn't hard," said Lionel.

Next year 3rd graders will be 4th graders and they can play the violin, viola and the cello.

By Jasmin

NEWSPAPER ARTICLE

This article was part of a newspaper unit taught in a grades 4–5 classroom.

Eleven-Year-Old Discovered in Army

A shocking discovery was made Wednesday at the Green Beret training camp in Oklahoma City. One of the lieutenants found out that recruit Jason Marks was only eleven years old. Reporters have had difficulty getting on the base because the army is trying to keep the matter quiet.

Alison Dalber from Madison, Wisconsin, had found out the story from her boyfriend in the same unit. Young Jason was discovered when a lieutenant had found his birth certificate and noticed that the year had been changed.

It is surprising that Marks passed the tests. He is tall and looks old for his age. He is also smart and muscular. The army must be embarrassed about the situation. I wonder where Jason will show up next.

LETTER OF REQUEST

Dear Mr. Bassett,
We the fifth graders need more food choices because sometimes third and fourth graders take all the good choices. I don't think that all the cafeteria's food is not good. I just think we need more good food. So please, please try to ask the cafeteria ladies to either make more of the good stuff or put two things out so we could just pick one or the other.
Thanks for reading.

Sincerely,
Jake

JOB APPLICATION LETTER

Dear Mr. Ron,
I want to be a conflict manager because I like to help my friends and little kids like in kindergarten when they need help. Also I want to be a conflict manager because I want kids to be safe and so you could stop writing referrals for kids this year.

Thank you.
Brenda

LETTER TO AN AUTHOR

October 4, 2001

2021 Forest Lane
Fayetteville, GA 30214

Dear Mr. Burch:

I am from Crestwood School in Madison, Wisconsin. Our reading group has read your book called *Ida Early Comes Over the Mountain*. We all loved it and wanted to write to you. We thought a sequel to your second book which I believe is called *Christmas with Ida Early* would be neat. We even thought up the title, *The Secret Life of Ida Early*. We thought that Randall or Ellen, or even the twins could find a ring in her bag while trying to write another note. Then tell of the supposedly strange man she was to marry. We don't know how this story will fit with your second book because we haven't read it yet, but I think we've got a good idea. We would certainly appreciate it if you would write back to us, but it would make us even happier if you used our ideas in your next book. Thanks.

Your new friend,
Jenny Brauer*

GREETING CARDS

The photo at right shows a display of Boss's Day greeting cards from students to their principal. ELLs wrote many of these cards.

*pseudonym

Greeting cards sent to the principal by students

IMPORTANCE OF SOCIAL COMMUNICATION

If I were ranking the chapters in this book by importance, this one would be near the top. Even though I see examples of high-quality writing in almost all classrooms I visit, I also see the absence or misuse of conventions everywhere. The most common transgressions are in letters to strangers who will probably judge the writers—and their teachers—by the fact that dates are missing and signatures are first names only. In my view, it is essential that work going public—and public means to one stranger as well as thousands—be acceptable in all its conventions. This rule should apply whether the writers are age six or sixty.

CHAPTER 6

Mixed Media

Over the past quarter century technological advances have made it easy not only to augment the written word with visual images, decorative print, and artistic layouts, but also to merge those media into a three-dimensional experience. At the same time, the traditional ways of enhancing text with drawings, photographs, calligraphy, and dramatic interpretation still thrive. All these forms of mixed media are suitable for classroom use, and they can be especially useful in mixed-language classrooms where ELLs at every grade level may have difficulty in understanding some written language or expressing their knowledge and ideas in writing.

TEACHING WITH MIXED MEDIA

One simple way that teachers can use mixed media productively is to add aural and visual elements to their instruction. Textbooks, the common source of content in classrooms, often present too much information too quickly and in technical language. Even in all-English classrooms, teachers find that they have to reexplain some textbook material in more simple language for students to understand. By using charts and diagrams to augment textbook presentations teachers can simplify and clarify the information students need.

At right is a visual aid one primary-level teacher uses to remind her students to include sensory and emotional information in their stories. The numbers she has written on the face represent seeing, smelling, tasting, hearing, thinking, and feelings, respectively.

After initial instruction, students can benefit

Reminder to include sensory information

from further presentations using mixed media. When they see pictures, charts, or diagrams, and when they play videos or audio recordings after their first exposure to new material they are better able to understand and remember what they have been taught.

For memorizing miscellaneous information such as definitions, names, and dates, aural forms of mixed media work better than anything else. Facts and words embedded in jingles, poems, and games stay with children much longer than words in isolation. For instance, many millions of children have learned the alphabet first—and permanently—by singing the alphabet song. Not only do young children thrive on aural patterns, older students and adults excel with them, too. A high school history teacher I know brings his guitar to class regularly to play little songs he has made up to define important concepts like freedom, democracy, and capitalism. His students sing along with him to memorize the definitions, and they seem able to call them up as needed. In my own experience, I still remember the songs, poems, and dramatizations I learned in my ninth-grade French class, even though I have long ago forgotten how to conjugate French verbs.

MIXED MEDIA IN ASSESSMENT

Mixed media can also play an important part in assessing children's learning. Teachers who put visual elements into some of their test questions find that ELLs do better on those questions than on strictly verbal ones. Those teachers also try to include some questions that can be answered with drawings or diagrams. On a fifth-grade science test, for example, a two-teacher team included items asking students to draw a diagram of the solar system and pictures that showed the characteristics of certain planets. Another teacher pretested her second-grade students on their knowledge of pond life by handing out sheets of paper with only a large empty pond drawn on them. By asking the children to draw all the creatures they could think of that might live in that pond, she got a much larger set of answers than if she had asked them to write the creatures' names. She was also able to see that many of her students thought of pond inhabitants only as fish, not as insects and birds, too. Their perceptions might not have been so readily apparent if they had only been asked to write out the pond inhabitants' names.

MIXED MEDIA LEARNING MATERIALS

An emphasis on mixed media not only changes teachers' instruction, tests, and children's learning habits but also broadens the range of instructional materials available to children in classrooms. Textbooks need not be the only—or even the major—resource for learning content. Instead, teachers can provide well-illustrated informational books, large posters that accurately picture animals, objects, places, and people, a store of science and social studies videos and, as far as possible, genuine artifacts or models of things that children are not likely to see in their own environment. In one classroom I visited, students had made papier-mâché models of exotic birds from photos taken at a zoo demonstration that could be used by other classes not fortunate enough to go on a zoo field trip. Making the models also helped the students remember the distinguishing characteristics of the birds they had seen.

MIXED MEDIA IN CHILDREN'S COMMUNICATION

So far in this discussion I have emphasized teachers' uses of mixed media, but from here on I will focus on how students can use media to support, expand, and demonstrate their learning. In this context I am going to ask you to think of human communication as a toolbox holding several different implements. As babies, children are able to use only the tools of physical movement, facial expression, and oral sounds to communicate with their caregivers. As they grow older, they add the tools of speech and, later, drawing. By the time children enter school, most of them have also added writing—or pseudo writing—to their repertoire. As they progress through their school years, children rely more and more on speaking and writing and less on other tools. To compare the communications pattern of a typical six-month-old child and a typical sixth-grade student, I have constructed a chart (right). My purpose was to emphasize the changes in tool use as children grow, not to represent the amounts of use accurately.

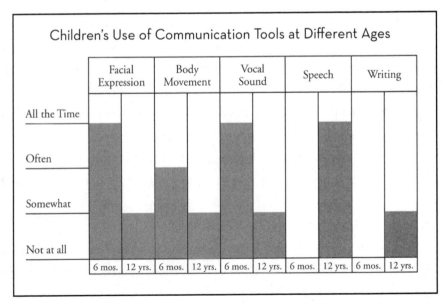

Children's Use of Communication Tools at Different Ages

The components of a chart of ELLs' communication are almost the same as those of native English speakers. The only differences are that some components are introduced later and their proportions change more slowly. Also, individual rates of change are determined largely by how long a child has lived in a second-language community and how long she has been in school anywhere. In working with ELLs, teachers need to consider individual patterns and provide for the use of various forms and amounts of supportive media as children gain competence in English. It might help for teachers to think about the extent to which any entering ELL uses speech or writing (in either a first or second language), body movements, facial expressions, and silence in classroom communication. Even a rough estimate would help them provide access to appropriate mixed-media activities and set reasonable expectations for their use.

SUPPORTING WRITING WITH MIXED MEDIA

At the same time, teachers need to look at what is already happening with—or without—mixed media in their own classrooms. If, like most classrooms, yours is writing oriented, ELLs and struggling English speakers are probably producing much shorter pieces than their class-mates, writing on the same safe topics over and over, or even making excuses to avoid writing altogether. If, in contrast, talking, drawing, singing, reciting, demonstrating, and dramatizing are accepted as regular components of the curriculum in your classroom, it is already a hospi-table place for ELLs to learn and to demonstrate their learning. In either case, what I can do to help you use mixed media more strategically is to suggest a range of activities and explain why they are suitable for students at different stages of writing competence.

DRAWING AS A SUBSTITUTE FOR WRITING

Teachers should recognize that drawing is a learning medium and use it as a starting place for expanding the use of mixed media for ELLs and other children who are not yet able to write much. Drawing works well, not only because all children like to draw but also because it is a medium available in all classrooms at all times. In the early stages of learning a new language, ELLs should be able to use drawing—as needed—as a substitute for writing in their note tak-ing, daily work, homework, projects, and tests. If you take the time to reassure your students that it's all right to draw an animal when they can't remember its name or to draw that animal eating or caring for its young instead of describing the process in written words, they will be able to give you a clearer picture of what they know. Although drawing is only the first step in using mixed media, it is one that will enable even beginning writers to participate in classroom activities and learn how to express themselves in literate ways. At right is a drawing of the life cycle of an insect by a primary-level ELL.

WRITING WITH SYMBOLS

Mixing symbols with words is an easy and practical way to communicate information. Teachers can use this technique when they make charts or write information on an overhead projector. In a unit on exploration, for example, you can draw a tiny ship, some waves to represent an ocean, a crowned head for a king, and a stick figure at the prow of a ship for an explorer. You can represent trading goods by drawing a chest with things in it. Never mind if the "things" are not clearly distinguishable; you can call them spices or gold or whatever you wish. Symbols can also be used in Venn diagrams to show how items are distributed. In the illustration at right, a first-grade ELL has made a Venn diagram with the things she likes in one circle, the ones her teacher likes in another circle, and the things they both like in the overlap of the two.

Life cycle of an insect

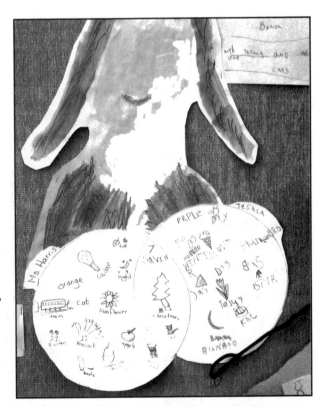

Self portrait and Venn diagram by Jesaca, grade 1

TEACHING WRITING IN MIXED-LANGUAGE CLASSROOMS

PICTURE SEQUENCES

Actually, a whole story can be told in a sequence of pictures. To present a story as a comic strip or a graphic novel, native English speakers and advanced ELLs can add some dialogue or a narrative to their pictures, while newcomer ELLs may use drawings alone. Although feelings and thoughts are difficult to convey in pictures, children can use the cartoon technique of adding facial expressions and thought bubbles to suggest them. At right is a story-planning sheet a first-grade girl wrote in comic strip form. When she showed her pictures to her teacher and told her the plan, they worked out some of the words she needed. Then the teacher wrote in the words you see included.

Story planning sheet by Andrea

LABELS, CAPTIONS, AND FACTOIDS

As ELLs become more comfortable in English, you can encourage them to start using writing more extensively with visual and oral media. Labeling their drawings is a natural step in this direction, since all children seem to use labels intuitively to make their drawings more understandable to others. In fact, I don't think I have ever seen a young child's drawing of his family that did not include labels identifying each family member. As children mature and let go of family labels, they continue to label unfamiliar objects, animals, and processes in their drawings. You can encourage this type of labeling by pointing out examples in informational books and by using labels liberally on your own posted charts and pictures. When it comes to labeling things in science, math, or social studies, where even the oral words are unfamiliar, you may want to sit down with a small group of ELLs and give them the words they need. Although the primary purpose of labeling is to build children's vocabulary and spelling skills, it also serves to gently push them into doing more writing. Here is a picture of a beaver, drawn and labeled by a primary-level child in a mixed-language classroom.

Labels used to describe a beaver

From one- and two-word labels, children can move on to writing captions that describe or explain a picture. The basic purposes of caption writing are the same as those for labeling, but captions also demonstrate understanding beyond just names and enable children to explain things that are not easily drawn, such as the functions of body parts. Below is a display of drawings by children in a grades 1–2 mixed-language classroom with captions giving facts about birds of prey.

The next step is the creation of some "factoids" to be pasted on posters or pictures. On a poster picturing an African elephant, for example, children could post bubble-shaped notes, each with a piece of information about that animal they learned by doing research. This tech-

Display of pictures and information about birds of prey

nique would also work very well for drawing parts of the solar system or maps of the world.

Using pictures regularly as the impetus for writing labels, captions, and factoids is a good general classroom practice. I would encourage you to put up a new poster, drawing, art reproduction, or large photo every week, whether or not it is connected to a unit of study. Then ask students to add one of the three kinds of writing described above. The picture you choose could be something as simple as a painting of a tree or something as complicated as a scale drawing of a race car.

BRINGING OTHER MEDIA INTO THE MIX

Drawing is certainly not the only medium readily available in classrooms. Children can also use spoken language and physical movement in conjunction with writing. An oral report easily lends itself to a written accompaniment in the form of an outline of the main points that can be displayed or distributed. A video can include written titles and explanatory bridges between its scenes. When a play is presented to an audience, a printed program listing the names of the actors and stating the time and setting is usually provided. However, since these mixed-media activities demand a fair amount of language knowledge and competence in other skills, I would use them only with intermediate-level students and only after they have had considerable instruction and practice.

MEDIA AS COMPLEMENTS TO WRITING

From using writing as a supplement to other media, ELLs should be able to proceed to using pictures, speech, and construction (see p. 68) as the partners of writing, with each medium complementing the other. When I mentioned having students draw in their journals earlier, I was thinking of the pictures doing nearly the whole job of communicating an experience. But what if, instead, each medium communicated its own share of that experience: the drawing presenting the factual information at one point, and the writing presenting what happened before or after or the writer's feelings about the experience? Such a partnership opens up the possibility of bringing new media into play. A child could bring in cookies he has baked at home for everyone to taste, explain orally how he made them, and then hand out copies of a written recipe. Another child could show off a stuffed animal she made, along with an oral explanation and a written version describing the materials and the construction steps. My first thought in suggesting these more complex uses of mixed media was to say—as I did above—

that such activities are really suitable only for intermediate students. But then I remembered seeing puppets made by first and second graders next to a display of their writings describing how they made them. These same children—the majority of them ELLs—had done another project in which they constructed models of their ideal bedrooms and then described them in writing. In both cases, writing came after the projects were constructed, which makes sense—the children had to work through the processes before they could explain them effectively in writing. Above and at right are two photos of the puppet project. The first one shows puppets on display, while the second is a close-up of one boy's explanation of how he overcame difficulties in making clothes for his puppet.

Puppets made by grade 1–2 children

> Alex
> Making clothes IS Tricky
> MY tricky Part was Putting
> the clothes on. I Solved
> the Problem by trying and trying
> and never giving up. Another
> Part was tricky too, the
> Pinning Part because It's hard to
> Pinn I Solved this Problem
>
> by aksing MY teacher to help
> Me.

Explanation of difficulties in making puppets' clothes by Alex

TEACHING WRITING IN MIXED-LANGUAGE CLASSROOMS

The picture I have of the bedroom construction is not clear enough to publish, but I can show you the writing that went with it.

My Dream House

Please come into my dream room. The T.V. is by the wall. I like to watch Sponge Bob Square Pants on my plasma T.V. My comfortable couch is in the living room and my computer is in the living room. I like to sit on my couch and play on my computer. My toy is next to my computer. I like to play with my toy. My ipod is above the T.V. I like to listen to my ipod. My bed is on the floor. I like to sleep in my bed. Goodbye, have a good sleep.
By Andy

THE IMPORTANCE OF LISTENING

Although listening is not exactly a medium of communication, it is a close partner to writing. Hearing someone else read your story after you have finished the final version can be quite an educational experience. All the things that you left out or didn't make clear—including spelling and punctuation—become apparent when another person stumbles over your words or looks confused about your meanings. I would make it a rule of thumb in classrooms that no written piece should be handed in before another person has tried to read it out loud to the writer.

STILL MORE MEDIA TO MIX IN

In laying out a path from drawing to writing and from writing to other media that fit readily with it, I realize that I have not touched all the bases of using mixed media in classrooms. I would like to complete this chapter by naming and explaining briefly some of the more sophisticated types of media that support and enhance students' learning.

ROLE-PLAYING AND DRAMATIZATION

Role-playing and dramatization are both powerful media. At the simplest level, a game of charades can help ELLs expand their vocabularies and gain a better understanding of the meanings of words they have already heard. At a higher level, students can combine their knowledge of spoken and written language with physical action to dramatize a story or re-create historic events. When I taught first grade many years ago, my class prepared a dramatization of

"Hansel and Gretel" to be presented before an audience. After listening to me read the story several times and discussing the events and characters' feelings, they improvised their own version of the action and dialogue. I'm certain today's ELLs could do the same. Still another possibility for informal dramatization is having students create scenes to present information they have gleaned from reading and research. A book I read long ago, *From Communication to Curriculum* by Douglas Barnes, persuaded me that having children act out the ways people lived in other times and places is the most effective way for them to understand and remember history and geography.

AUDIO RECORDING

Students who find writing difficult can also use audio recordings to facilitate small-group discussions, oral reporting, and the presentation of research. In these situations, the children do all the work assigned except for writing things down. By speaking into a recorder they can preserve their thoughts and information for the teacher and other students to hear or for themselves to transcribe later on. Alternatively, audio recordings work very well as substitutes for written reports for ELLs and other students who have difficulty in writing them out. Recording also offers the advantage of preserving performances over time so they can be compared with later ones to show students' growth.

Another valuable way to use audio recordings is for stories that students want to hear again, either because they didn't catch everything the first time or just because they liked them. ELLs, especially, expand their vocabularies and sentence structure by listening to stories over and over. Stories are certainly better teaching tools than lists of words or sentence drills. Finally, a recording can serve as a surrogate for another person who reads a student's work aloud while she listens. Even when reading their own work, students make errors that are apparent to them when they hear their own voices hesitate, misread, or sound puzzled.

CONSTRUCTION

Earlier I mentioned student-made replicas of papier-mâché birds, but there are many other things that ELLs can construct from various materials that will consolidate and display their learning. We have all seen models of volcanoes, covered wagons, and American Indian homes in classrooms, made by students at home as projects culminating a unit of study. Usually these are rough representations of reality that add little to the knowledge of the creators or the viewers. Instead, I would like to see more realistic and complex constructions done in classrooms to help students, especially ELLs, understand what they have heard and read about in a unit.

Media can be mixed by having students explain their constructions visually and in writing. At right is a drawing by a student in a grades 1–2 classroom, illustrating how she made joints for one of the puppets shown earlier.

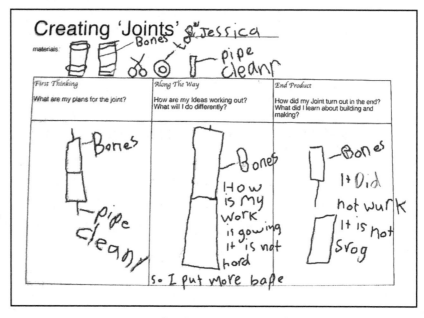

Description of making puppet joints by Jessica

PowerPoint presentations are easy enough for older students to learn how to make, and they effectively combine images and print to go along with an oral report. Young children will certainly need some help from an adult in doing the computer parts. The advantage for ELLs is in being able to report orally with some support from print and pictures.

VIDEO

Videos can be made with a computer or a camera. The advantage of using a computer is that you can gather the images you need from all over the Internet and mix them with your own filmed material, drawings, and print. Many middle school and high school students are already making videos under their teachers' direction or on their own. I recently saw two excellent videos made by students. The first one was done by sixth graders to inform their peers and parents about the abuse of child workers in the chocolate industry in Africa. The video used images from the Internet, student voices giving information they had garnered from research, and a printed call to the audience to buy chocolate products from companies that did not use abusive practices. In the second video, a class of high school students just sitting in their seats was the major image throughout. No one spoke, but one after another, smiling, healthy-looking students held up signs with short messages opposing teen use of drugs and alcohol. This video was a simple but effective use of mixed media. The demands of both videos, I think, could also be met by elementary-level students under the guidance of a technologically adept teacher.

RETHINKING OLD HABITS

Expanding the use of media in your classroom is akin to opening new doors through which your students can move out and explore the world. Too often we take the traditional classroom so much for granted that we don't realize what a small, confined, and isolated venue it is. We don't think about how its traditional book, pencil, and paper tools might constrict learning and expression, or how the schedules, rules, and rituals we devise to keep order preclude spontaneity and creativity.

CHAPTER 7

Popular Culture

Although we all know there is a popular culture that young people are very much involved with, that culture has not, for the most part, infiltrated the classroom. Officially, most teachers take the position that there will be no popular music, no jokes, no raps and, most recently, no text messaging in class. The thinking behind these unwritten rules seems to be that since popular culture operates on lower standards than academic culture, or perhaps on no standards at all, it would corrupt student learning if it were allowed into the classroom. Left unbridled or kept clandestine, popular culture might do just that. But I would argue that teachers can use popular culture to expand and enhance the school curriculum for all students and especially for ELLs, who are just as likely as their English-speaking classmates to know it and love it. Moreover, I believe that in the real world, popular culture often merges with serious entertainment and important communication to produce works of value. I will add—in a whisper—that the merging of popular culture with the school curriculum might increase student engagement in all classroom activities.

At the same time, popular culture can be a support for ELLs and other students who need help with writing. Because so much of popular culture is visual, oral, and patterned, and because children are at home with so many of its manifestations, it serves as a supplement, a complement, and even a replacement for the formal written language they often find difficult and dull.

FORMS OF POPULAR CULTURE

For the purposes of teaching writing in mixed-language classrooms, the question is this: How can teachers use popular culture to support and advance student writing? My list of forms of popular culture for supporting writing at the elementary level is long but only suggestive. And I must add that my advanced age and the rapid changes in the world of popular culture may mean that some of what I have listed is already old hat and that other forms your students know well don't appear in my list because I haven't heard of them yet.

- Chants, raps, and cheers
- Cartoons
- Movies and their characters
- TV shows and their characters
- Catch phrases
- Jokes, puns, and riddles
- Comic strips and comic books
- Playground games
- Fashion fads
- Songs, jingles, and rhymes
- Graphic novels
- Bumper stickers and vanity license plates
- Slogans from TV commercials, billboards, and signs
- Advertisements
- T-shirt messages
- Celebrity gossip
- Popular toys
- Gadgets
- Instant messaging
- Sports
- Video games

GETTING STARTED

If you feel unprepared after reading my list, join the crowd. Most adults are not up to date on what young people are thinking, doing, and talking about. Still, because you are teachers, you need to have at least a nodding acquaintance with the world your students live in. You could spend some time watching their television shows, listening to their music, reading their magazines, and looking at their Web sites. Or, if that process seems too slow and, perhaps, too hard on the nerves, you could let your students lead the way by inviting them to bring their popular culture interests into the classroom.

Because many teachers include a discussion of current news events in their daily schedules, this could be a place to talk about the happenings, people, objects, and messages students are drawn to. Or you might begin to open some bits of classroom time to different forms of popular culture and see what happens. I'm thinking about allowing students to choose rainy-day games, bring in music CDs to be played during silent reading, spend time at approved Web sites when their regular classwork is finished, and read their favorite magazines at independent reading time.

Another approach you may feel more comfortable with, because it is more easily managed, is to have a pop culture time once a week (or once a month) during which students may "show and tell" about anything that fits into a designated category, such as comic books or video games. If you decide to do that, I would advise planning ahead with students so that the classroom is not flooded with more items than can be handled on one day, and to ensure that nothing violent or inappropriate is brought in.

I've saved the best approach for last. If you still have an up-to-date library and a librarian at your school, they may prove to be a treasure trove of popular culture for your students—and you. Arrange to have your class spend time in the library regularly, not only to browse among the books, but also to plunge into the materials and electronic media you don't have in your classroom. You'll see that the magazines in the library are not limited to the likes of *National Geographic* and *Ranger Rick*, as they used to be. Now they cover the range of young people's interests from clothes to music to video games, and some of them are in the major native languages of the student population. As for books, there are graphic novels, which you may have heard about and looked at, but could not get for your classroom. Today's school libraries also have their fair share of informational books that are not just about animals, olden times, and electricity, but also about hip-hop, graffiti, and skateboarding.

If you are lucky, the librarian I just mentioned is now a freshly prepared "multimedia specialist" with all the expertise that title implies. But even if he is still the same school librarian who's been around for years, like you he has been involved in professional development, read books and journals in his field, and gone to professional conferences. He knows a lot more about popular culture than he did in the past and about how to teach it to students. Finally, there are laptop computers in the library that are up to date and connected to the Internet, so under the media specialist/librarian's supervision, your students can go to exciting and useful new Web sites and interact with the cream of popular culture.

In the best of all possible worlds, you and the school media specialist will be able to team up to plan instruction and activities for your class. As yet, you may not know how to make PowerPoint presentations and videos, but the specialist does. He can teach you and your students at the same time. He can also show them how to find information for their reports, look up the bios of their favorite celebrities, and obtain the addresses of organizations and people they'd like to contact. Although you may still be your students' writing teacher, the media specialist can show them how to use computers to correct, add to, and revise their writing on the computer. And to their delight, he will teach them how to embellish their writing with decorative touches, illustrations, fancy fonts, and even music. He knows a few tricks, such as "wordles" that enable students to perform magic with their writing. A wordle, in case you don't know, is a "word cloud" made up of the words in an ordinary piece of writing. A computer program reproduces words in different sizes, depending on how many times the word was used in the original writing. You can also use different fonts and colors for different words. Since I can't explain wordles any better than I've just done, at right is an example of one done by a fourth grader.

A work by Odalis, grade 4

ADAPTING POPULAR CULTURE FOR CLASSROOM USE

Back in your old-fashioned classroom, your students will still be able to use forms of popular culture in their writing. In connection with the classroom curriculum, students can create rhymes, slogans, or mnemonics to help themselves remember math or science terms and processes or historic names and events. They can write songs or chants that contain content-area information. For language arts they can create cartoons with captions to illustrate events at school or home or write new dialogue for existing comic strips.

At the same time, popular culture can be used to promote students' self-esteem and their sense of community. I'm thinking of such activities as making vanity license plates as name cards for student desks, writing a gossip column with themselves and their classmates as the celebrities in it, and creating a T-shirt slogan that proclaims the class's identity. The following vignette gives some idea of the scope of possibilities in an ordinary classroom by describing how one teacher has assimilated popular culture into her curriculum.

In Sally Wells's fourth-grade classroom, popular culture plays a significant role in reading, writing, social studies, science, and math. For example, Mrs. Wells teaches a unit on baseball that leads students to decorating their own baseball caps and inscribing slogans on T-shirts. Later in the year, the study of a science unit on native forests produces a logo that students also put on their T-shirts. In math the students make poster board strips of their own first names using measurements and then illustrating and defining the mathematical terms on those signs. Here is one of them:

On an ongoing basis, there is a weekly game called "Wear Words Wednesday." In preparation for that day, students select words from a book they are reading or other classwork that is relatively new to them and, perhaps, unknown to other members of the class. Students write their words on one side of an index card and their definitions and sentences on the other side. They wear their word cards on a string around their necks all day Wednesday, so other students can see them and ask about them. During a special period that day each student presents his or her word to the class and explains it.

Another ongoing practice is a set of computer activities involving a stuffed animal that is the class mascot. This animal—a lion the class has named Leo—is one of several produced by a company that links its products to computer doubles, their imaginary environment, and their activities on its Web site. These inexpensive stuffed animals can be purchased at local stores, and from then on the owners (in this case, the students) have free access to the company's Web site by using the code number that comes with each animal. On the Web site the doubles play, work, exercise, eat, dress, bathe, sleep, and travel at the direction of their owner(s). By engaging in educational games, students can earn play money to spend on clothes, toys, or furniture for their doubles. They can also keep them happy and healthy by giving them attention, feeding them nutritious foods, and having them participate in exercise. The students can also write messages to their animal doubles.

The students in this class have become very involved with their mascot's double and take every opportunity to give it loving attention. In addition to the computer activities, Mrs. Wells has used the students' interest in their mascot by having them write to and about it.

Below is a shared writing by Mrs. Wells's previous class. You'll notice that they had a different class mascot with a different name than the one in the vignette.

In January our teacher bought a class pet for our room. It wasn't what we were expecting. We thought it was kind of a joke, and then it was the coolest thing ever. She bought us a stuffed animal called a Webkinz. It was a dog, just like we said we wanted and had voted on. We named it Dragon.

Mrs. Wells placed Dragon in a lunchbox with a journal that had our password and code in it. Each weekend one of us would take Dragon home. We took Dragon to our soccer games and read to him. We visited the virtual Dragon on the computer. We wrote in the journal all about our weekend adventures. We learned that if we didn't have a computer at home, we could use a computer in the school library or at the community center.

Sometimes during rainy day recesses, we visited Dragon in the Webkinz virtual world and earned more points. It was fun to buy him things and take care of him. Some of us started buying our own Webkinz and began sending gifts and messages through the Webkinz world. We had so much fun. Dragon turned out to be the best class pet ever!

As fads wax and wane, the forms of pop culture you choose to use in your classroom will change. Without knowing the future, all I can do is describe some ways of using forms of popular culture that have been around for a while and are still pleasing young people.

CREATING ADVERTISEMENTS

In our world, advertising in one form or another is all around us. By borrowing bits of well-known television commercials and print advertisements and altering them to suit our own purposes, we make them part of the popular culture. I still remember a parody of the Pepsi Cola jingle that my friends and I sang 50 years ago. We didn't create it, but we certainly helped make it popular at our school.

Although musical jingles aren't so prominent anymore, certain slogans capture the public imagination and get widely used. Almost everybody knows the origins of "Got milk?"; "I could've had a V8"; and "What's in your wallet?" and finds them funny in new contexts.

I observed the "What's in your wallet?" slogan in a series of commercials created by students in which one person asked that question of a stranger who then pulled out of his wallet an unlikely object, such as a pair of socks or a can of soda, and proceeded to tell the television audience why they should buy that item and carry it around with them. In another classroom, students produced commercials around their own invented slogans. One phrase, used to advertise fast food was, "Yum, yum, yummy. Put _____ in your tummy!" Another was, "Quicker than a wink, cleaner than a whistle!" advertising a kitchen cleaner. More interesting than the slogans the students produced, however, was their appropriation of the language and situations found in real television commercials. Clearly, they knew how the genre worked. This appeared to be true of their print advertisements also. Here is one ad created by a fifth-grade girl who studied print advertisements on her own.

> Nothing good to eat? Too cold to go out? Tired after work? Expecting guests and don't have time to get to the store? Then your hunger and worries are over!
>
> Call Moresworth Fast Delivery Store and tell them your grocery list.
> In less than five minutes your special order will arrive from Moresworth on an underground conveyer belt directly to your home. It could mean a lifetime without grocery shopping and it saves time.
>
> Call Moresworth today or send a letter enclosing a date on which the workmen can come and install your conveyor belt.* A $100 deposit is required.
>
> *Not available in Alaska or Hawaii

One fifth-grade class got so absorbed in the field of print advertising after collecting and critiquing real newspaper and magazine ads that they wrote and illustrated their own ads for imaginary machines that kids their age might be interested in. While reading real ads and making their own, they also decided to create a glossary of elaborate names for ordinary objects that advertisers might use to deceive the public. For help in finding big words for small things they used a dictionary and a thesaurus. Below is part of their glossary, followed by one student's ad.

Discarded particles pusher	Broom
Rotating blade mechanism for growth retardation of botanical specimens	Lawn mower
Intelligence growth facilitator	Teacher
Horizontal terrestrial representation	Map
Time duration informant	Clock
Mid-anatomy suspension device	Belt

Pet Reducer

We have the solution for all the people whose pets have grown too large. Here's what you can do with dogs that take up a whole chair and cats you can't cuddle with!! Our new invention will shrink your pet to just the right size for you. With only two buttons—"start" and "shrink"—you can reduce your pet in just one minute.

Order now for just $10. Take your oversized mastiff and watch him shrink to the size of a Chihuahua!

CREATING COMIC STRIPS

For a long time, superheroes have been a strong interest of children and teenagers. Comic books first introduced them more than 60 years ago. Then came TV shows, movies, and dolls; next, video games and computer games; and, most recently, graphic novels. Although the number of superheroes has expanded considerably, the old favorites, such as Superman and Batman, still have a strong following. Because superheroes are so familiar to children, including ELLs, teachers do not have to spend time developing a context or stimulating interest. Students need help only in ways to express their knowledge and interests in writing.

Grades 1–2 teacher Emma Harris has successfully used superheroes in a writing activity for some time. Her procedure is to have students think of themselves as superheroes by creating a name, an image, and an arsenal of superpowers. Students begin by making a labeled drawing of their superheroes in costume along with visual representations of their special abilities and how they use them. Then students create a story based on a formula that includes a problem, a villain, a struggle, and a victory for the hero. The story is laid out in a series of boxes, just like a comic strip, with a narrative below and some brief dialogue written in bubbles that come out of the characters' mouths. To support her students in this activity, Ms. Harris creates her own superhero, "Super Teacher," and a comic strip, demonstrating her work step by step as she asks her students to work on each part of their strips.

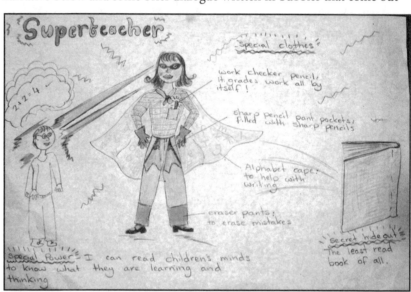

A teacher's labeled drawing of a superhero

JOKES, PUNS, AND TONGUE TWISTERS

Other forms of popular culture that children like are jokes, puns, and tongue twisters. When it comes to writing those forms, however, English-speaking students find it much easier than ELLs. Getting the humor in jokes and puns often depends on understanding that many words have more than one meaning, as author Lynn Truss demonstrated in her recent book, *Eats, Shoots & Leaves*. Teachers can ameliorate the difficulties for ELLs by reading aloud such books as the Amelia Bedelia series by Peggy Parish (continued after her death by her nephew, Herman Parish), and *The King Who Rained* by Fred Gwynne, which illustrate the humor in word ambiguity. At the same time, teachers must recognize that it takes a lot of language knowledge to be able to appreciate or create puns and jokes.

Nevertheless, in observing mixed-language classrooms I have found that all students can write certain types of jokes if there is a prototype they can use as a model and lots of teacher demonstration. One such familiar prototype is "Why did the chicken cross the road?" A third-grade class whose teacher read them many chicken jokes came to understand that the fun was in answers that give no real reason. Here are three of the best jokes they produced:

Why did the chicken cross the road? Because the light was green.
Why did the chicken cross the road? Because it needed exercise.
Why did the chicken cross the road? Because his mother told him to.

Knock-knock jokes are harder to write, but the same class produced these after hearing a lot of them from their teacher and watching her demonstrate how they are constructed.

Knock, knock.
Who's there?
Will.
Will who?
Will you play with me?

Knock, knock.
Who's there?
Happy.
Happy who?
Happy birthday.

In addition, here are a few tongue twisters written by fourth graders. The only supports they needed were a sheet of popular tongue twisters, the class word wall, their vocabulary knowledge, and—when all else failed—a junior dictionary.

Little lambs like luscious lettuce.
Freddy Fox fixed fifty-five French fries.
Watching whales while weeping wildly, Wilma waded where waves washed.
Clumsy cats catch curious catfish.
Six sisters sewed seven silk sundresses.

Finally, at right is an example of a humorous restaurant menu for Halloween that uses puns.

RAPS AND SONG LYRICS

Although musical jingles, mentioned earlier, are no longer popular with children, music and rhythm still are. Outside of school, your students sing along with their fa-

RED GLOBSTER

APPETIZERS

French Flies
Onion Things

BREAKFAST

Scrambled Legs
Stack of Ghost
Sugar Handcuffs
Mice Crispies
Corn Snakes

BEVERAGES

Grim Coffin   Killer Beer
Blood Wieser   Mountain Ooze
Extra Bloody Kerry

GOUPS

Cream of Mushed Rooms
Oyster Goup

MAIN CORPSE

Deviled Hand
Globster with Drawn Butter
Spaghetti and Feetballs

GREASY GRIMY GHOUL CONTEST
Rub Web

An example of a humorous menu

vorite artists and rap along with their favorite rappers. Most of the actual songs and raps are too complicated or inappropriate to be models for school writing, but the genres themselves can be used. When it comes to rapping, most teachers have to let those students who know how to do it lead the way, first making sure that the rappers understand what may and may not be said in school. Once the rest of the class gets the hang of it, some students may be able to create their own raps, but doing that does require a special talent. Songs will probably come from the teacher, and all students are capable of creating new lyrics for simple songs. The teacher needs to choose songs that are not only appealing to the age group, but also have strong repetitive patterns, which usually means folk songs, nursery rhymes that have been set to music, and old traditionals. Here are just a few songs that seem to work with elementary students:

This Old Man
There's a Hole at the Bottom of the Sea
The Bear Came Over the Mountain
Jingle Bells (the chorus only)
Merrily We Roll Along
Here We Go 'Round the Mulberry Bush

One teacher I know taught her class to sing a song that was popular among adults almost a hundred years ago. Here is the original lyric:

K-K-K-Katie, beautiful-Katie,
You're the only, only girl that I adore.
When the moon shines over the cowshed,
I'll be waiting at the k-k-k-kitchen door.

This song appealed to the children because they could put their own names in it and change the last line. Out of consideration for the boys, whose names didn't fit as well as the girls' names and who wouldn't like to be "adored," the teacher composed an alternate version:

B-B-B-Brandon, terrific-Brandon,
You're the only, only guy who knows the score.
When the bell rings in our classroom,
I'll be waiting by the yellow school bus door.

Using these models—and words their teacher suggested when they were stuck—the students were able to write their own verses that the class added when they sang the song. Although the student example below shows only small variations from the model, it represents a solid beginning at writing song lyrics.

C-C-C-Christy, lovely Christy,
You're the only, only friend for me.
When the sun shines over the school,
We'll be sitting under the big oak tree.

In presenting these examples, I don't want to imply that writing song lyrics is easy for children. Although they seem to be able to find rhymes for one-syllable words without too much difficulty, they have a much harder time with putting the correct number of syllables in a line. Singing the songs does help by letting them hear the number of musical spaces that have to be filled. Classes that sing and recite poetry regularly do much better at writing in these forms.

VIDEO GAMES

Video games in themselves don't fit into a classroom curriculum or help students with their writing, but there is emerging research suggesting that video games can stimulate an interest in reading and writing. Perhaps because of that research, some publishers of books for children and adolescents are pairing their books with games, expecting readers to play and players to read. At this point I am not suggesting that teachers create units around video games, but I think they should not entirely ignore them either. Since so many of your students are playing these games at home there may be ways to capitalize on their interest. So what I do suggest is encouraging older students to write about the games they play—in blogs, strategy guides, and notes to other game players. You might even want to organize a video game club that would no doubt attract both kids who hate to write as well as good writers. In addition to the activities I've just suggested, members could design video games with pictures and writing, describing what their characters would be like, what the story of the game would be, and where and when it takes place, etc. Since I have only played video games once or twice—and that was a while ago—I can't be more specific about the writing involved.

TWO MORE EXAMPLES

I can't leave the topic of pop culture without sharing two more examples of student writing that don't seem to fit in anywhere else. Both are illustrated books explaining in detail how today's children like to spend their free time. The first is entitled *How to Break Dance* and the second is *How to Do Your Hair*. Both books were written by ELLs in a grades 1–2 classroom. Below are pictures of the books' covers followed by the full text of the breakdance book.

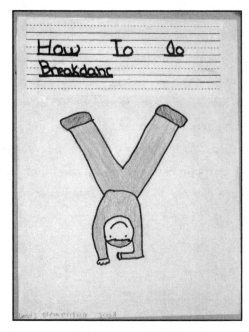

Book cover by Yanik

Book cover by Diana

If you want to dance cool read this book. Break dancing means to dance cool cool cool.

First you do a handstand. You put your hands down on the floor. Your head is down too. I like dancing.

Then do the spin to be cool. Then spin on your head.

Next do the back flip to be cool cool cool cool After that do a spin on your feet to be the coolest.

Later do a spin. You jump on the wood and spin with all your body.
Finally you end up with a nice set of movings. Here you are! You just danced the coolest dance called the break dance!
At the end you deserve a rest. Are you broad? You did a good job

By Yanik

WRAPPING UP POPULAR CULTURE

Although I have not provided suggestions for using all the forms of popular culture I listed at the beginning of this chapter, I am going to stop here. My list contained everything I could think of that might be used for classroom writing at the elementary level, but the reality is that I haven't seen all of them tried out in classrooms, and I don't have student examples of everything I have seen. In addition, I hesitate to lean too heavily on forms dependent on electronic media because those media are not available to all children, either in their classrooms or at home. So, in a very real sense this chapter is unfinished. I leave it to you, creative and resourceful teachers, to use this chapter as a starting point for experimenting with all the forms of popular culture your students know and like and then to write up what you and they have done. I would be thrilled to find out that you have gone beyond my tentative efforts.

CHAPTER 8

Academic Writing

Looking at the title of this chapter, you may wonder, "Haven't we been dealing with academic writing all along?" Well, yes, in a way. All the types of writing discussed so far were selected for their appropriateness as school activities and usefulness in building students' writing skills. But what I have in mind now is writing specifically connected to subject areas, such as answering questions, summarizing, and writing reports. These kinds of writing present new challenges for students because they are different from the informal, personal writing they are familiar with. Yet for many ELLs who have missed those years of schooling in which English vocabulary, sentence structures, and conventions are taught, there are additional challenges, so extra supports are necessary.

To address the topic of academic writing, I begin by presenting some general strategies teachers can use to help smooth out the bumps in the road for their ELLs, and then I move on to suggested activities suitable for all students at various grade levels.

EXTRA SUPPORT FOR ELLS

Provide work partners for your ELLs for new or difficult academic tasks. Choose native English speakers who are academically competent, enjoy playing teacher, and don't mind carrying the burden of additional work. The role of a partner is to explain the task at hand and demonstrate how to do it through his or her own writing. Partners must also be generous, asking only that their ELL partners contribute whatever they can.

Get into the habit of accompanying your verbal instructions with generous doses of drawings, diagrams, and demonstrations of what you want students to do. Don't assume that any of your students know how to write a social studies report, for example, even if you're sure last year's teacher taught that. Before giving a new type of assignment, demonstrate it and provide guided practice. By then you will know whether you have to do more intensive teaching.

Present standard formats and common sentence structures for traditional assignments, such as question answering and report writing. Also remind your students that putting their full names and the date on a homework assignment is a routine they will be expected to follow throughout their school careers.

Assign some writing tasks that are already partly done. In asking students to take notes on a science experiment performed in class, for example, write out the first two or three notes yourself, explaining why you chose those items, and ask students to write only three more. With unfamiliar or difficult tasks, you may want to start out by providing beginning sentences for several paragraphs or even offering a fill-in-the-blanks format.

Provide an organizing structure for recording information. A teacher-made grid such as the one pictured below is clear, easy for students to fill in, and useful for studying afterward. It is particularly helpful for ELLs because of its clear and uncomplicated form and its modest demands for the amount of text.

Keep writing tasks brief. I think this is a good rule of thumb for writing assignments for all students in the elementary grades. What we really want is quality, not quantity. Brevity is even more important where ELLs are concerned. When a task is too daunting, students of any background may give up without trying or comply minimally by copying a section they do not understand from a book.

Ask English-speaking students or experienced ELLs to reexplain your instructions to the entire class. They are more likely than you to use language that all students can understand.

If ELLs understand instructions well enough but have only a sparse English writing vocabulary, allow them to do an assignment in their own language or with labeled drawings or diagrams, but also encourage them to insert English words and sentences wherever they can.

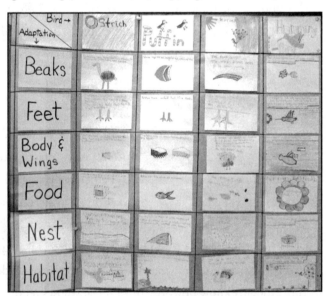

A grid for organizing information about birds in teacher Mary Brown's classroom

Make an oral and visual presentation of new vocabulary words a part of every content-area unit. When you present new words, be sure to explain and/or demonstrate their meanings; don't count on students understanding dictionary definitions. Review vocabulary words frequently, point them out when they come up in text, and expect students to use them in speech and writing.

WRITING IN THE PRIMARY GRADES

For beginners, whether in kindergarten or first grade, the first writing tasks involve transcribing letters and numbers legibly from models the teacher provides and then remembering them well enough to write them without models. Although these tasks are primarily practical, they are also academic because they require visual discrimination, deliberate memorization, and exact replication. The next step is reproducing words, especially one's name. Ensuing academic tasks involve figuring out the spelling of words not memorized and writing numbers in the proper order. From there children are expected to apply their basic knowledge of words and numbers to composing short sentences and matching numbers to appropriate contexts, such as groups of objects, clocks, and calendars. Usually, the academic goals for kindergartners are to be able to write all letters of the alphabet legibly, all numbers from one to ten, several common words, and short sentences related to their own experiences.

It's hard to think of these rote tasks as stimulating activities, but children seem to find them satisfying because at last they are able to do what they have seen adults and older siblings do. Yet there are ways of turning them into games or real communication experiences that will encourage children to go beyond teachers' assignments and do them independently.

WORD CARDS AND GAMES

Many games can be played using word cards. To play, children need their own packs of cards on which they write all the words they know. Also included in the pack are teacher-written cards with a few important "connecting words," such as *the, and, to, a, has* and *is,* and lots of blank cards for adding new words. One game, led by the teacher, has children making sentences with their cards; another is laying out all the words beginning with a certain letter. A third is laying out people words, animal words, or thing words. The object of all these games is to lay out as many words or sentences as possible in a given length of time. After learning the games, a child can play alone or with a partner. Although the games do not involve actual writing, they encourage children to create as many new word cards as they can in order to do better the next time they play.

Word cards can also be used for authentic communication. Children can lay out messages they want to send to a friend or family member. Once the sentence is complete, they may copy it on special decorated paper, put it in an envelope, and address it with a name. An appointed post person delivers all the letters within the classroom; students deliver their own family letters.

LANGUAGE EXPERIENCE

Besides playing card games, children can "write" simple narratives in kindergarten and first grade. Early in the school year their writing is really dictation, but it approximates writing because of its language style of complete sentences on one topic. Although many teachers consider a dictated story finished work, others ask children to make their own copies so the story will be truly theirs. This type of composition is modeled on the "language experience" approach to

reading and writing introduced by Roach Van Allen in the 1960s. Children recount personal experiences that are important to them, and a scribe writes them down just as they are told, without correcting grammar or word choice.

It is interesting to note that the overwhelming majority of kindergartners—including ELLs—I have observed are able to dictate their ideas in complete sentences without being coached, even though in later grades the same children may relapse into run-ons and fragments. I would guess that they are able to compose sentences because the stories that have been read and the things the teacher writes on the board are always sentences. At right is an example of a story that one kindergartner dictated to his teacher. Because the teacher

Dictation and writing by Raul, a kindergartner

Teaching Writing in Mixed-Language Classrooms

is bilingual, he is able to take dictation from Spanish-speaking students, and write it out for them in whichever language they prefer. This piece shows the child's dictation followed by his own attempt to write it in English.

WRITING ON THEIR OWN

As the year goes on, kindergartners gradually move on from dictating to writing on their own without any specific instruction. Although some will not make it past a few words with inventive spelling in this grade, others will be able to produce short texts by themselves. An ELL wrote the thank-you letter reproduced below in October of his kindergarten year. Before the class wrote their letters, their teacher had led a brainstorming session and written several words and phrases that children had suggested on the board. This boy's letter is his final copy, produced after an editing session with his teacher. He was able to expand on the class's suggestions without help. Moreover, most of the spellings and all the handwriting are his own. I must point out that this boy is quite intelligent and not a newcomer. No other child in the class was able to duplicate his accomplishment so early in the year.

Thank-you note by Eliseo, a kindergartner.

USING THE CALENDAR

Since primary-grade teachers ordinarily teach a calendar routine for learning numbers, names of months and days, and weather terms, the daily calendar time is a good opportunity for children to learn to read and write single words. Although teachers start the school year by writing calendar information themselves, first graders and some kindergartners can soon copy those words legibly. After a while, a teacher could ask a few of her best writers to make new word cards for the official classroom calendar. The fact that there are twelve months, seven days, and five to ten short words to describe weather gives every child an opportunity to have his or her writing displayed on the class calendar more than once during the school year. For practice, children can fill in monthly personal calendars to keep in their rooms at home.

SIGNS AND LABELS

Another simple writing task is making instructional signs, such as "Wash Hands." First graders are certainly capable of deciding which signs are needed and selecting the right words for them. For math, they can form numbers and write them out as words. For science, they can learn to write labels for pictures of animals. If social studies involves knowing the names of specific places in the community, they can make labels for those and paste them on a large community map hung in front of the room. In one classroom I visited, the teacher made cutouts of a house that read "_____ lives here." Each child filled in the blank with his or her name, and the teacher pasted the houses on the community map, too.

WRITING IN GRADES 1 AND 2

First and second graders continue all the types of writing activities they began in kindergarten, expanding the length, spelling accuracy, vocabulary, and sentence structures they are able to use. Typically, only newcomer ELLs and struggling English speakers are still allowed to dictate their pieces to a scribe. Most primary-grade writings are personal narratives, a continuation of what they wrote in kindergarten. Strictly speaking, these are not academic writing activities, so I will not address them in this chapter, but they do have an academic effect by increasing children's writing skills.

INFORMATIONAL WRITING

At the same time, primary-grade children are beginning to do informational writing that requires some fundamental research, organization, and recording skills. The proliferation of attractive, accurate, and content-rich informational books for children in recent years has made it possible for children to go beyond the superficiality of geography books and the technicality of encyclopedias. Informational books introduce children to a world of people, animals, plants, places, and objects they would otherwise know nothing about. They also expand children's vocabulary by giving names to the things introduced. Most important, however, informational books enable children to do academic writing in the forms of labels, captions, and reports. At right is a science-report cover created by an ELL in a grades 1–2 classroom, based on a class study of the solar system along with the text of her report. Although the author does not give much information about planets, she fills in well with her imaginary adventures as an astronaut.

Astronaut book by Diana, a grade 2 ELL

> Hello, I am astronaut Diana. I am kind. I have a special belt. The belt plays music for me. I have special boots. The boots are cool because they have a special button. When I push the button, the boots turn into fire boosters. I have a big "D" on my suit. When I take the "D" off, a string comes out. When the string comes out, I can swing on it to another planet.
>
> I live on planet Blue. My coordinates are (A, 4). The best of all is the food . . . it is blue! On planet Blue, it is cold and soft. Today I have a mission. I am going to Earth. It is far away from here. I am going to get water and bring it home.
>
> On my way to Earth, a strange thing happened. I heard a sound. It was strange. My rocket was freezing. I was on a big ice land. I turned on my engines and I flew away.
>
> I passed a planet. Bad water came out. The rocket power was not working because water went in the engine. I was scared, but my big rocket flew faster, and I got away from the bad water planet. I was close to Earth.

INFORMATIONAL BOOKS IN THE PRIMARY GRADES

Since children who are just beginning to read may not be able to read informational books on their own, you can read them aloud. But even when children can read, it is a good idea to lead them through the process of finding, selecting, recording, organizing, and presenting information. In the vignette below, I describe how a teacher and a school librarian collaborated to teach the fundamentals of research and writing reports early in the school year before the children could do much reading or writing.

Joyce Davidson's first graders have become interested in whales through an article she read to them from the local newspaper describing the yearly migration of humpback whales in the Pacific. The children want to know more about whales, but there is nothing available in the classroom collection of books. Realizing that the school library will have what her classroom lacks, Ms. Davidson consults with Karen Austad, the librarian, hoping to borrow some books about whales to read to her class. Instead, Ms. Austad suggests a joint project that would involve a small group of children in doing research and presenting a report to the class.

The next day, when five class volunteers report to the library to work with Ms. Austad, she is ready with three books that have sections about whales, a file of photographs, and a large pad of newsprint paper set on an easel. After she and the children seat themselves at a low table in a corner of the library, she asks them what they already know about whales. Not only do the children remember information from the article their teacher read, they also know things they've heard elsewhere. Ms. Austad writes down everything the children tell her on the chart under the heading "What We Know," and then reads it all back to them. Next she asks, "What more do you want to learn about whales?" The children pepper her with questions, and she writes them all down under the heading "What We Want to Find Out." The children ask,

- ❖ "Why aren't whales fish?"
- ❖ "How much does a whale weigh?"
- ❖ "Do they sleep?"
- ❖ "What do they eat?"
- ❖ "Where do they travel every winter?
- ❖ "How do they breathe?"
- ❖ "What are their babies called?"

To try to answer the children's questions, Ms. Austad reads short sections from the books she has selected and shows the photos in her file. She also takes time to explain the hard parts of the books and any new vocabulary and allows the children to ask more questions. Although the books tend to repeat certain facts, she doesn't skip anything. Repetition will help the children remember the most important points. When Ms. Austad has finished reading, she takes a new sheet of newsprint to write the report the children will now dictate to her.

Not surprisingly, the children's interest has shifted from weight, habitat, and food to the fascinating subject of how whales breathe. As the children report back in their own words what they've heard and seen, Ms. Austad writes down that whales are mammals, have lungs, breathe out through a blowhole in their heads, can stay under water without breathing for about an hour, and cannot stay long on land because their lungs get crushed from their body's weight. Although the children would like her to write more, she tells them this is enough for a report. She reads aloud what she has written and then has the children repeat it all in chorus, one line at a time.

Back in the classroom, the children "read" their report to their classmates, adding other information from memory as they go along. Later everyone will copy it to take home and read to his or her family. As the year goes on, other groups of children will have this research experience in the library, and Ms. Davidson will adapt the process of listing what children know and what they want to find out for other topics as she reads new books to them and they increase their own ability to read for information.

Although the early research groups in this classroom did not actually do the reading and writing involved in creating a report, they learned a great deal about how to do research and how to turn information into a report. These are important academic skills they will use and develop further throughout their school careers.

As children become true readers and writers, the process described in the vignette changes considerably. With many books and articles available in both the library and the classroom, teachers can design whole units around types of animals, plants, places, or people and expect children to read widely and gather a broad spectrum of information. By the time they are in the third grade, they can complete a grid like the one pictured on page 86 and use it to write longer and more sophisticated reports, illustrate them, and label their illustrations accurately.

DESCRIPTIVE NARRATIVES

Another type of writing commonly done in primary-level classrooms is the descriptive narrative. Teachers often ask their students to describe a field trip they took, a holiday with their families, or a school event they participated in. Although this type of assignment is appropriate for children of this age, the results are often disappointing to read. The problem is a lack of detail. Children tend to write that they did this or saw that, but do not truly describe anything or give any flavor to the experience. If, instead of the general direction to "write about" something in the past, children were asked to give their full attention to a specific object or process in the present and to describe what happens to it in a short period of time, they could do a much better job. A good place to start might be to have a couple of children at a time watch the class hamster for a few minutes in order to write about his appearance and his actions. In good weather, the whole class can go outside to observe birds, bugs, or squirrels and write about them afterward. If you have a digital camera, you can take photos of those creatures to help children recall what they have seen and note details that they might not have observed at first.

The key to getting this kind of detailed writing from young children is having them do the observation first and write about it immediately afterward.

Below, one boy describes what happened when a small boa constrictor got loose in his classroom. He wrote this description right after the incident.

> One day we were petting the Boa Constrictor. I said we should put him away, but his tail was in the sofa. While I was loosening the tail, his head went into the birdcage. His body was stuck.

> Carmie was scared of the snake and went looking for the janitor. Bill was sad because the head was stuck in the bars of the cage. Mrs. Proctor was sad too. I was scared that the snake was stuck in the cage.

> We got it out very slowly. While we did that his tail went around Bill's leg. Mrs. Schten had to lift Bill's foot into the snake's cage and unwind the snake from Bill's leg.

THE THIRD-GRADE SHIFT

For most children, third grade is a turning point in their education. Some easily navigate the shift; others do not. What has been called "the fourth-grade slump" really happens in third grade, but does not become apparent until the end of that year when standardized test scores are reported out, or the beginning of the next year when textbooks take over the curriculum. In third grade, multiplication is usually introduced with its demands for memorization. Children can no longer use counters or their fingers to figure out the answers to math problems. Social studies that used to be about their neighborhood and the people they know now deals with places and people far away or long in the past. Science, which once meant getting familiar with interesting animals and their lives, now means studying rocks called igneous, sedimentary, and metamorphic. Best—or worst—of all, there are now tests and homework assignments in these subjects that include writing. These changes represent the beginning of formal academics that many children are not prepared for at age eight.

ANSWERING FORMAL QUESTIONS

Although the full written pieces children are asked to do in third grade are much the same as what they did in the primary grades, tests and homework require something new: writing answers to questions. In the primary grades, worksheets and workbooks asked only that children circle, mark, match, or write single words. Now they are expected to demonstrate their knowledge with complete sentences and sometimes paragraphs. To further complicate matters, children also meet a new set of question words, such as *explain*, *name*, and *describe* that don't sound like questions at all.

The best advice I can give for supporting your students in answering questions is to demonstrate and give them lots of oral practice before they meet these new expectations in homework and tests. It also helps to get into the routine of giving practice tests before the real ones. Go over these with students afterward so they can see what they know and don't know, but more important, where they may lose out because they misinterpreted a question or did not answer it fully.

MORE HELP FOR ELLS

Again, I want to add some special advice for supporting your ELLs. For the first time, they will be expected to write sentences with a formal structure and include the technical vocabulary of content areas. Here are some suggestions:

1. Form temporary, small groups for those ELLs who are having trouble so they can get some extra demonstration and practice.

2. Go over textbook questions orally before assigning them. Ask ELLs to rephrase questions in their own words. Explain any words they don't understand.

3. Partner ELLs with English-speaking students for textbook assignments early in the year or whenever they are having trouble.

4. Design tests that are student friendly by keeping them short, supplying a vocabulary list they can pull words from, putting easier questions first, and asking questions that can be answered in one brief sentence.

5. On a test, include some questions that can be answered by drawing pictures or diagrams.

6. Allow ELLs to substitute words from their own language when they do not know the English words.

GOING ACADEMIC IN THE INTERMEDIATE GRADES

In grades 4, 5, and 6 children are expected to continue improving their existing writing skills and to branch out into various types of academic writing. For the first time they are asked to take notes on textbook chapters, summarize what they have read, and produce reports and essays. In stating these facts, I do not endorse all that takes place in classrooms; I merely recognize its existence. In the primary grades, teachers generally have a great deal of control over the components of the curriculum, its activities, and materials. They decide what is appropriate to the needs and interests of their students and make adjustments as necessary. In the intermediate grades, the topics and goals of the curriculum are set at the district or state level, and often the instructional materials to be used also are selected there. Those materials, authored by external "experts" may be content rich and logically structured, but they are divorced from the realities of the classroom and its living inhabitants. The best thing teachers can do is to adjust some aspects of the curriculum and the materials and devise activities that fit their students better than the ones in commercial programs. Let's look at some of the techniques teachers can use to support their students through the challenges of academic writing.

NOTE TAKING

Note taking is a difficult transition for students because it requires selecting what is important in a text or a teacher presentation, and selection is a high-order thinking skill. I remember that even in college I often took down too much or too little of my professors' lectures and became frustrated when it was time to study those faulty notes for a test. Eventually my friends and I figured out that one solution to the problem was to study together, sharing our notes and our memories. That worked, but I'm not sure I ever got better at note taking.

Intermediate elementary students can also benefit from study groups when preparing for a test. But as with me, group support won't make good note takers out of poor ones. Not only do children tend to take down too much, they also copy some sentences word for word. To help your students improve their note-taking skills, you have to provide some specific instruction. The first step, as always, is teacher demonstration. Children need to see how their personal "expert" performs a skill in order to get the general idea. While you are demonstrating, think out loud, letting students know why you are making certain choices. Afterward, give them a sheet with the original text and your notes, so you can go over it the next day and answer any questions.

After seeing some demonstrations, students, as always, need practice. Start with a short paragraph that has a number of facts in it. Have students read it twice silently, and then put it out of sight so they cannot copy anything word for word. Next, ask them to write notes that will help them remember the important points in the paragraph. Students don't need to use sentences or even words in their notes. Drawings, symbols, and abbreviations often work just fine. To test the effectiveness of their notes, have students return the original paragraph to you and use just their notes to answer your questions about it. Repeat the questioning part of the exercise a few days later. Although remembering the paragraph will help some students both times, good notes should make a difference for everyone. Don't grade this exercise or ask students to report how they did; let them be the judges of their own notes.

Afterward, whenever you ask students to take notes on an article or a book chapter, do some random collection and assessment of those notes. Tell your students that you are looking for accuracy, brevity, and their own words. You might award an imitation medal—as a humorous touch—to the student who wrote the most concise set of notes.

SUMMARIZING

Summarizing is actually just one step up from note taking. Students who have learned to take good notes find it relatively easy to turn them into sentences and combine those sentences into a paragraph. Nevertheless, you should demonstrate the technique orally and in writing with short articles or stories and then give opportunities for practice.

Starting with oral practice is best. To build students' competence, routinely ask about short sections they have just read. Other students may offer additions or corrections in a helpful way. Not only does this activity improve students' summarizing ability, it also helps ELLs to comprehend information they may not have fully understood the first time.

For practice in taking notes and writing summaries, students can do an activity called "Read, Talk, and Write." It goes like this:

❖ The teacher assigns a book chapter or an article to be read. She has broken it into segments that take about two minutes each to read.
❖ Students of similar abilities work in pairs. They read only one segment at a time.
❖ Partners tell each other what they have read.
❖ Both students write down the information they think is important in note form.
❖ They repeat the process until they have finished the assigned piece.
❖ Partners read each other's notes.
❖ Both partners write summaries of the whole piece and share them.

The power of this activity lies in the brevity of each work segment and the sharing of information and decision making between partners.

INTERMEDIATE REPORTS

The essential difference between primary- and intermediate-level content area reports is quantity and coverage. Intermediate teachers expect their students to write longer papers and include subtopics with details. Usually they have them do research and write as individuals. My personal view is that intermediate students, especially ELLs, still benefit from group work on reports, not only because the better writers and researchers can help their classmates, but also because assignments can be differentiated to fit students' interests and abilities in a group situation.

LEARNING TO USE A RANGE OF RESOURCES

If students have learned the basics of research, note taking, and summarizing, the greater demands of intermediate level reports should not be daunting. The only new things they have to learn are how to seek information from a broader range of resources and how to organize longer reports. For teachers, the main job is teaching more sophisticated research techniques than the ones used in the primary grades. Because no one will be putting the right books in students' hands or Web sites at their fingertips, they will have to figure out where and how to find what they need. Typically, students stumble at two points in the research process: not knowing what the most important print resources are and not being able to generate enough key terms to use when looking for information in books or on the Internet. To educate your students about the first stumbling point, begin the practice of doing research for fun on a regular basis. In the vignette below, one teacher who had no student computers in her classroom used bulletin board quizzes to teach her students how to use reference materials effectively.

Johnny and Ben are working on the bulletin board quiz their teacher, Marlys Sloup, posts every week in her grades 4–5 classroom. Although they have until Friday to hand it in, the boys take pride in being among the early finishers with all the right answers. Besides, some questions are tough and take a lot of thinking and searching.

This week there are four groups of questions. The first group is about the local "Bicycle Month" soon coming up. It includes questions about scheduled events, bike safety, theft prevention, and bicycle rentals. The second group of questions concerns a pie graph illustrating water distribution around the world. The students have to compare water availability in certain countries, pick the most surprising fact on the graph and tell why it surprised them, and explain how human behavior affects water supply. Next, there are three "Winnie the Pooh" comic strips with the question, "Is Eeyore an optimist or a pessimist? Explain why you think so." Finally, a group of questions focuses on the West Coast states of California, Oregon, and Washington. Students have to identify major products, earthquake zones, find the name of the deepest lake, and give one state's nickname.

Like many of their classmates, Johnny and Ben are attracted first to the comic strips. Reading them through, they readily see that Eeyore always expects the worst to happen, but they don't know whether that means he is an optimist or a pessimist. Clearly the place to go is the adult dictionary on the shelf by Ms. Sloup's desk.

To answer the water questions, the boys first study the graph itself. Then they have to go to the world atlas to find out where the countries listed are located. The text under the graph tells them that only five percent of the earth's water is fresh, which is certainly the most surprising fact. The atlas also helps them answer some of the questions in the geography group, but they have to consult the encyclopedia and almanac in the library for the rest. Because they still don't know the name of the deepest lake on the West Coast, they Google it on one of the library computers and quickly find out that it is Crater Lake in Oregon.

The Bicycle Month questions send them back to the classroom to search copies of the local newspaper that Ms. Sloup keeps on a rack. They have to look through several days' editions, but they know to go first to the "contents" boxes on each edition's front page to locate particular articles. Those articles answer most of the questions, but not the ones about safety or bicycle rentals. Fortunately, Johnny remembers that there is a poster on bicycle safety hanging in the library, so back they go. While there, Ben recalls a recent lesson they had on using the Yellow Pages in the phone book. They go to the phone books the librarian keeps on a shelf and, sure enough, there is half a page of bicycle-rental places listed. The boys write out all their answers and hand them in. Surprised at their speed, Ms. Sloup tells them they are the first ones to complete the quiz this time.

KEYWORDS

Generating keywords that will lead to information about a topic is difficult because it requires a large vocabulary, some background knowledge, and imagination. Too often students run dry after searching for the topic word and don't know how to go deeper. As usual, I suggest the best way to begin teaching this skill is with a teacher demonstration and guided practice. Some practice can take the form of a game: have students list as many keywords as they can think of for a particular topic in a given period of time and see who can come up with the most.

Two other strategies will also help students generate keywords: going first to a general reference source, such as an encyclopedia, to read about a topic in general and taking down as many subtopic words as they can find; and second, being on the lookout for keywords in all sources that may lead them to new sources. The additional benefit of going to a general source first when doing research is that students get an overview of a topic that helps them understand all the subtopics and details they may later find.

ORGANIZING NOTES

Another challenge in doing research for a report is keeping notes organized. Inexperienced students have the tendency to fill up note cards for every source, thus repeating information they already have and clustering information by sources rather than subtopics. When the time comes to separate pieces of information, they have to rewrite them somewhere else. To overcome this problem, teachers should offer their students a homemade notebook for taking notes, with at least one page devoted to notes for each subtopic. To help students get started, teachers can give them some of the headings they will need or brainstorm them with the whole class.

BENEFITS OF COLLABORATION

Because actually writing a report is a different process for every student, and because each of these processes is long and complicated, I cannot give you an all-purpose strategy for supporting students through this complex task. But I can remind you that collaboration is the best support for all students in this type of work, and I can show you the notes, summaries, and the report produced by two fifth-grade boys who had worked through the note taking, summarizing, and research activities I've suggested. They were part of a larger group that was studying life in America in the early part of the twentieth century.

General Stores

Student 1's Notes

Lots of General stores, 1920s and 1930s

Kept records and bills at long wood desks

Sold all kinds of things

Things for families—food, clothing, school supplies, medicines, farm
equipment, shoes, no bread

Coffee grinder

Food came loose (not packaged in factories)

Services—clerks wait on people, carried things out, climbed ladders, scooped
out unpackaged food

Student 2's Notes

General stores before 20th Century

Sold food, clothes, shoes, drugs, equipment

Sold pickles, etc., in bulk

People ground their coffee

Clerks did all the work

Baked bread at home

Summary 1

In the early twentieth century, most people bought almost everything they needed from a general store. General stores were located near the center of a town or a community. Clerks did all the work. They put things up on shelves and took them down for customers. They candled eggs to make sure they were okay. They carried out heavy packages a lot of the food was sold in bulk, It was not in packages that came from factories, Boxes and barrels held flour, salt, sugar and pickles.

Summary 2

Before there were a lot of cars people did their shopping in a General Store. General stores carried almost everything, including clothes and equipment. Many things were sold in bulk. You could grind your coffee on a big red coffee grinder. The clerks would take things off the shelves for you, scoop pickles out of the barrels, and fill your shopping bag. They also delivered things to your house. People made their own bread at home.

Full Report

In the 1920s and 30s you could probably find everything a family would need in a general store near your house. The general store had many canned foods on high shelves behind the counter and glass display cases filled with candy and many other things. It also had a big red coffee grinder. You cranked the coffee turning a big handle and out came your ground coffee.

Lots of things that general stores sold came in bulk. That means that big barrels or containers hold things like flour, salt, pickles, peanut butter, sugar, corn meal, cookies, and crackers. Clerks had to scoop out what the customer wanted from the bulk containers and measure it. Then they put it in a cloth or paper bag. General stores also sold dry goods, like men's women's and children's clothing, shoes, harnesses, school supplies and medicines.

Clerks had many jobs. They had to use a ladder to get some of the items down from the tall shelves. They also had to candle eggs. Candling eggs is when you hold up an egg to a light and look through the egg to see if it is good or not. Clerks also carried out heavy packages for people who had cars. Some of them delivered groceries to people's houses on a bicycle.

A lot of people ordered groceries over the telephone and said, "Charge it." They paid at the end of the month. The store owner had a big wooden desk where they kept their bills, etc., and figured everything out.

One thing people didn't want to buy was bread. They were embarrassed to buy it because everyone thought you should make your own bread.

In many ways this report is unlike the usual geography or history report intermediate students are asked to write. I chose to reproduce it here because the notes, summaries, and full report were short enough to be used as an example, and the other types of reports I have were not. I chose it also for the novelty of its topic, one that intermediate-level students find far more interesting than usual historical topics. Finally, I chose it because the research method the writers and the rest of the class used was unconventional. Although they did some book research to get an overview of the topic, their main resource was interviews with older people in their families or communities.

I want to add an example of a more traditional type of report, cautioning you that although it appears more learned than the one on general stores, such a report is really much easier for students to do because all the information in it can come from a single book.

The Castle in War

In case a war should start, many things were done to protect the castle. One of the things was making arrow slits. These were made so soldiers could shoot their arrows and be protected. To insure safety for the castle, walls were made very thick so even battering rams had a tough time. Workers also made openings in the walls so missiles and rocks could be dropped on the enemies. Another thing they made was called a portcullis. It was to block the opening to the castle.

If any of the enemies should get caught between the towers they were showered with arrows and missiles. These were dropped or fired through openings above called murder holes.

The most common weapons then were crossbows, mace shields, battle axes, swords, bows and arrows, daggers, and spears.

WRAP-UP

As I end this chapter, I am aware—and probably you are, too—that two forms of writing traditionally considered part of the academic curriculum, formal essays and book reports, have not been touched on. Their omission is deliberate. In my opinion, teaching the structure and conventions of the formal essay is not appropriate in the elementary grades, and book reports should be taught as creative writing rather than academic writing. For these reasons, I have omitted the first type of writing from this book altogether and included the second in Chapter 10, which discusses various types of imaginative writing. Read on and see why.

CHAPTER 9

Personal Narratives

Having children write personal narratives has become the predominant writing activity in elementary classrooms over the past several years in the belief that all children have interesting experiences and that writing about them requires no specialized knowledge or skills. Despite this rationale, the results often make dull reading. Young writers tend to plow the ground of ordinary vacations, common school field trips, and everyday visits to the supermarket over and over without raising any crops. Why? The answer, I think, is not that children have no interesting experiences to write about, but that they don't know which ones to choose or how to craft them into a compelling story. Sadly, it seems that these hindrances are more typical of ELLs and underprivileged children than of their middle- and upper-class peers. When they are asked what they are going to write about, these children often say, "I don't know," meaning, "I don't know what you want of me," "I don't know what is appropriate to write about," and "I wouldn't know how to present my story if I had one." If pushed to put something down on paper—and these children are pushed every day—they will produce perfunctory versions of the same old stuff or pieces that proclaim how much they love their families and friends.

THE PROBLEM AND THE SOLUTION

Harsh as my comments may sound, they are not meant to demean students' intelligence or native abilities. They are a criticism of those freewheeling writing programs that fail to familiarize children with the raw materials of writing and fail to provide them with the tools to turn those raw materials into interesting and authentic narratives.

A LICENSE TO WRITE

Before getting into the nitty-gritty of teaching personal-narrative writing, I need to explain the idea of "license." Almost all children are schooled by their parents in correct public behavior: what they may or may not say or do in public and what personal details are not to be revealed to strangers. The restricted words, behaviors, and events are not necessarily bad, but as far as parents are concerned, they are private. It shouldn't surprise you to learn that the scope of privacy varies from culture to culture, not only among racial and ethnic groups, but also among socioeconomic groups. Although children don't say so to their teachers, their sense of family, cultural, and personal privacy carries over to their writing, making them unsure about the propriety of addressing certain topics, recounting certain events, or using certain words. As teachers, we have to respect students' boundaries—even when we don't know where they are—by not urging them to tell personal stories they feel hesitant about.

To overcome the problem of children feeling they have nothing to write about, many teachers encourage them to keep a "writer's notebook" in which they jot down interesting ideas, words, phrases, and images that come to them at odd hours and in unexpected places and to refer back to their notebook during "writing workshop" at school. Such a notebook may work very well for adult writers and mature, well-organized students, but I doubt that it is compatible with the personalities and habits of most children. They are too busy living and learning about the world to mull over words or to write anything down. The raw materials of personal narratives have to be unearthed and made visible to children when it's time to write.

THE RAW MATERIALS OF WRITING

The question is, what are the raw materials that writers need? They are:

- ❖ A complete and coherent story
- ❖ Complementary details
- ❖ The voice of the narrator

Stating these raw materials, or elements, in formal terms may make them seem more special than they are and the writings produced more literary than they have to be. A complete and coherent story can be about something as simple as taking the dog for a walk, as long as the writer recounts what she and the dog did on that walk in some reasonable order and detail. Nor should students feel that they have to include everything; describing a few key details helps the reader to visualize the story. Bringing voice means that the writer puts a bit of his or her own personality into telling the story, letting the reader know "This is not just anybody's story, it is mine!"

TAKING THE FIRST STEP

Getting children to write compelling stories about their own experiences begins with showing them how others have written about theirs. Although you can use writings by past students, they are likely to be too individualized to inspire everyone in the class. I think better sources are professional writings about experiences common to all children. My all-time favorite as a story stimulus for primary-level children is the book *Alexander and the Terrible, Horrible, No Good, Very Bad Day* by Judith Viorst. I have never seen a classroom where this story did not excite children, moving them to recall their own "no good" days and write about them. In case you don't remember the book, it tells of Alexander, the youngest of three brothers, who recounts all the things that went wrong for him on an ordinary day. Like any child, he attributes most of his problems to the malice of his brothers and the thoughtlessness of his mother. Interestingly enough, for our purposes, the book is highly patterned in both structure and language. There is even a refrain at the end of each short episode when Alexander, out of frustration, says, "I think I'll go to Australia." In response to this stimulus, most children go on to write about their own bad days, although a few choose to write about a good day, instead. Out of the many writing examples I have based on this book, I have decided to show you three, all by second graders. The writers did not title them.

When I woke up, Sasha, my dog gave me a million licks. I really liked that!
I knew it was going to be a supercalifragilisticexpialidotious, very good day.

When I got out to the bus stop, I was the first one there.
I knew it was going to be a supercalifragilisticexpialidotious, very good day.

When I took my spelling test, I got all the words right.
I knew it was going to be a supercalifragilisticexpialidotious, very good day.

When I went out for recess three of my friends wanted to play with me. I said, "We can all play together. OK?"
I knew it was going to be a supercalifragilisticexpialidotious, very good day.

When the bell rang I was the first person in line to go in to school.

****

My mom, Dad, and I went on a camping trip where almost everything went wrong. When we had just gotten to the camping grounds and finished setting up the tent, it collapsed, so we had to do it all over again.

Then we went to fish in the lake and a big fish pulled me in. The same fish did the same thing to my Mom. We climbed out of the lake soaking wet and covered with seaweed and mud. When we took a shower and got really soaped up, the water turned cold.

After that, we went on a nature walk, and I tripped on a stick and fell flat on my face in the mud. When we had dinner the portable table broke and we had to eat on the ground.

At eight o'clock we went to unzip the tent so we could go to bed, but the zipper was stuck. My dad lifted the tent up and we went under.

In the morning we ate breakfast and packed up to go. We started driving home and got a flat tire. My Dad changed the tire and we finally got home.

****

Last summer I was riding my bike in the rain. I was going down a hill fast because the street was slippery. My bike fell over when I was applying the brakes. My leg got stuck in the spokes, and I couldn't get it out. I knew I broke my leg because I couldn't move it. My dad saw me fall, and he took me to the hospital.

When I woke up I had a cast on and my dad was with me. I stayed in the hospital for three weeks. My mom or dad came every day. It wasn't fun, and lots of times it was boring. The worst was when I had an itch. Then my dad would pour powder down my cast.

After four weeks I got crutches, but I couldn't use them very well. So then I got a walker. When school started I had to go with my walker. I used the walker for two weeks, then I just limped around.

My teacher said I was the best sport she'd ever seen. Now I walk just fine.

MOVING BEYOND IMITATION

The strength of *Alexander* as a model is the charm with which the author presents ordinary events. Its weaknesses—as a model—are its repetition and sparse detail. Because the structure of *Alexander* is episodic, even without the repeated language and refrains, children who base their writing on it also tend to write episodic undetailed stories, like the first two stories above. There comes a time, even with young writers, when teachers want their students to write about one experience in depth and detail, so they need a different kind of model, one that describes a single incident more fully. One such book for primary-level writers is *Owl Moon* by Jane Yolen, a richly detailed story of a child who goes on a nighttime walk through snowy woods with her father to look for owls. This book describes one adventure through words and pictures in extensive detail, making an uneventful experience exciting.

Relating to Other People's Stories

Although your students may not have gone owling with their fathers, most have had a special moment or a special trip with one of their parents, and that is what they should write about. Many primary-level books are similar, describing incidents that your students have not experienced but can relate to. To help them see those relationships, you're going to have to do more teaching than with a book like *Alexander*, which translates so directly to children's lives.

Strangely enough, many fairy tales and fables are easier to relate to than modern realistic fiction because they are thinly disguised lessons meant for children. "Beauty and the Beast," for example, helps children to understand that people's appearances are not always expressions of their characters. The fable "The Tortoise and the Hare" shows them that dedication and hard work count for more than flashy talent. "rumpelstilkstiltskin" teaches them that they shouldn't make promises they aren't willing to keep. When children have the opportunity to talk about the lessons in these stories, they can often find similar stories about themselves or people close to them.

Picture Books and Chapter Books

To help you get started using fictional models for real-life writing, I have listed several books below, grouped into two categories: picture books and chapter books. My reason for separating them is to alert you to their differences, which require a different approach to teaching. Unlike picture books that tell one story, chapter books tell many short stories that make up the lives of their characters. This complexity is fine for writers who are mature enough to develop one strategy with an overall message, but it can overwhelm novice writers. Teachers who want to use chapter books should pick out only one chapter or one short section to use as a model for writing. A further difficulty in using chapter books is that their stories are often unrealistic, putting ordinary children into extraordinary circumstances and attributing to them extraordinary wisdom and skillfulness. It takes a lot of teacher guidance and student thinking to distill the essences of everyday life from their depictions of grand adventures.

Picture Books

Ira Sleeps Over by Bernard Waber

The First Grade Takes a Test by Miriam Cohen

Nappy Hair by Carolivia Herron

Chrysanthemum by Kevin Henkes

A Piece of Home by Sonia Levitin

Who Belongs Here? by Margy Burns Knight

Amelia's Road by Linda Jacobs Altman

Margaret and Margarita by Lynn Reiser

The Relatives Came by Cynthia Rylant

David Gets in Trouble by David Shannon

Sledding by Elizabeth Winthrop

Sam's Worries by Maryann Macdonald

The First Day of School by Toby Forward

A Tooth Story by Margaret McNamara

Chapter Books

Does Third Grade Last Forever? by Mindy Schanback

The Stories Julian Tells by Ann Cameron

Amber Brown Is Not a Crayon by Paula Danziger

Rules by Cynthia Lord

The Year of the Dog by Grace Linn

Tuck Everlasting by Natalie Babbitt

The Circuit by Francisco Jimenez

From the Mixed-Up Files of Mrs. Basil E. Frankweiler by E. L. Konigsburg

Seedfolks by Paul Fleischman

Clementine by Sara Pennypacker

The Summer of Riley by Eve Bunting

Ida B . . . and Her Plans to Maximize Fun, Avoid Disaster, and (Possibly) Save the World by Katherine Hannigan

PROMPTS FOR THINKING

With children who have had some experience writing personal narratives, a brief prompt can bring forth memories for them to write about. Prompted by a sentence stem such as "It's not fair when . . .," children can think of many instances when something happened that seemed unfair and use those instances to complete the stem. But because we'd like them to do more than just write a number of unrelated sentences, ask your students to choose only one instance to develop into a story that illustrates why they feel as they do. Below are a few stems to help you get started, but you will probably be able to think of others that fit you own students' backgrounds and interests better than these do. My only caution is to beware of very general stems such as "I am happy," which is likely to bring forth only generic experiences.

I had a good time when . . .

I am pleased with myself when . . .

It hurts me when a friend . . .

I feel lonely when . . .

I get angry when . . .

I get bored when . . .

I laugh when . . .

I work hard when . . .

After some discussion with her teacher, a second-grade ELL chose the last prompt to recount her experiences getting ready for Christmas. To help her include details in her narrative, the teacher had her draw pictures of separate events related to the holiday and paste them into her journal. As you can see from the picture of her journal pages at the top of page 112, the teacher also supplied the spellings of some words that the writer could not manage on her own.

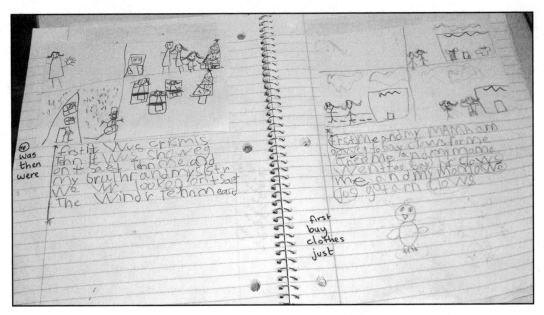

A story planning notebook of a second-grade ELL

A somewhat different prompt that also works for primary-level children and ELLs is "What brings out the angel (trickster, dreamer, good friend, complainer, show-off, etc.) in me?" When offering this kind of prompt, you should encourage children to use it as story title rather than a sentence starter so it won't inhibit the development of a full story. Nevertheless, the only examples I have do show it only as the beginning of one long sentence. Maybe you can get better results.

> If I'm almost asleep and my brother turns on the radio and says, "I can do my homework better with this on," that brings out the monster in me!

> If I'm running to catch the bus and the driver doesn't see me so I miss it that brings out the monster in me!

If you decide to use sentence stems or titles as prompts for intermediate students, you can avoid this problem by introducing them as devices for thinking; they do not necessarily appear in the body of the writing. Have students brainstorm ideas before deciding on one incident they want to write about. As a prewriting activity, prompts work best with partnering. Partners share their ideas and question each other about their experiences before putting them in writing.

VISUAL "QUESTION MARKS"

Another type of prompt for intermediate students is the "visual question mark." Obviously, this term refers to things that can be seen, but the objects, people, and scenes that fit the term are also mysterious, calling out for an explanation that a personal narrative can provide. So just any object, any picture, any pleasant outdoor scene won't do; teachers need to pick their visual question marks carefully. The following personal narrative was written by a fifth-grade boy after he studied a picture of a younger child building a sand castle on the beach. Something about the child seemed tentative. Instead of being fully absorbed in his work, he was gazing out to sea as if wondering what the future of his creation might be.

> I saw a boy on the beach. He was building a sand castle. I watched him as he made the towers. I watched him as he built the entrance and the room for the court to meet.
>
> About 4:00 he decided to go, and I went to see the castle close up. I could just see the knights and King Arthur ready for battle. Their worst enemy was the drastic sea.
>
> Soon the beach was empty, not a soul around, so I knew the war would begin. First the sea shot a wave that hit a tower. Then a bigger wave hit and a wall fell down. All was quiet. The sea was smooth and the castle was gone.

The fact that this personal narrative is fiction does not diminish its quality or its individuality. As we read it, we hear the story in an ordinary event, see everything we need to see in the few details, and get a strong sense of who the writer is, his knowledge of King Arthur and his court, and his feelings about the impersonal power of nature.

TELLING MY SIDE OF THE STORY

One last prompt for intermediate students that I'd like to mention is "My side of the story," a writing in which two people are at odds about some everyday matter. Although this prompt can be handled in various ways, all reflecting the challenges of being a kid, I particularly like the humorous monologues presented on the next page. To have her students express adult-child conflicts through monologues, the teacher asked them to imagine a conversation they might have, but to write only their part of it. In addition, she realized that she had to urge them to use the kind of kid language they would normally use in such a conversation. "How would you really say that?" she continually asked. The final trick to these monologues was to make one person's words suggest what the other person had said without quoting him or her. Here are two of many delightful monologues the students produced.

Bye, Mom!

The bus is coming.

I'll do that when I get home.

How come you make Jennifer's bed?

Why won't you make mine too?

    I can hear the bus coming.

I like my bed to be messy.

    It makes my room look lived in.

The bus is coming up the road!

    I promise I'll make my bed when I get home.

    Bye now.

    Mom, I think I need a ride to school

******

I don't like tomato juice.

I won't drink it!

If I do, I'll throw up.

Maybe even die.

Last night I could have . . .

Well, never mind.

I tried to give it to the dog,

But he wouldn't drink it.

Neither would the goldfish.

Today they were floating on top.

So Mom, I'm not drinking it either.

ROLE-PLAYING IN PERSONAL NARRATIVES

Looking back over the student examples I have collected over the years, I remember that the elementary-level writers I've known seemed to like writing the narratives of other people—

real and fictional—better than writing their own. Maybe that had something to do with their reluctance to reveal personal matters or their conviction that their own stories were not all that interesting. In any case, the narratives they produced about others were often longer, more interesting, and better crafted than the ones about themselves.

Here is an example of a student interpretation of another person's story. In it, a fourth-grade girl steps into the shoes of Red Riding Hood's grandmother.

Today is a beautiful day with the sun shining, but I can't get out of bed with this cold. I can't get any rest either because the woodsman is chopping down trees and making so much noise. No one is coming to visit me today way out here, and I'm too weak to cook my own meals. The food Little Red brought me last week is almost gone. I think it's time for me to move into town. As soon as I'm better, I'll leave these dangerous woods.

Yesterday I was lying in bed when I heard someone knocking at the door. I asked who it was and the voice said, "Little Red." Although the voice didn't sound like her, I was so glad to have a visitor I told her to come right in. But instead of Little Red, it was a wolf!

Fortunately I managed a scream before the wolf pounced on me. The woodsman heard my scream, and came running. He killed the wolf before it could gobble me up. Being attacked by a wolf in my own house is the last straw! I have had it with these woods!

Tomorrow I will ask my daughter to help me move to town where I can have my own little house and garden and people nearby. Maybe I can sell the extra produce I grow at the town market. Best of all, there will be no wolves!

HISTORICAL NARRATIVES

In Chapter 1, I presented some examples of student writing connected to a simulation unit on the adventures of pioneers traveling west on the Oregon Trail. While working on that unit, intermediate students do a lot more writing than I showed. Typically, their teachers ask them to keep diaries of people whose identities they have assumed as part of the unit. Because these people are fictional, their diary entries reflect the fictional events built into the unit. But the unit is also accompanied by some diary entries of real pioneers, so teachers may ask students to write entries for them. That way, students are pushed to follow more closely the language and conventions of the times. A third activity some teachers use is to have students keep diaries for characters in the historical fiction they read while working on the simulation unit. Below are excerpts from all three kinds of student diary entries, labeled for identification of the source.

Simulation Diary Entry

My husband Jack just said, "We're moving west!" We talked over our plans. By the way, my name is Bonnie. I'm 28. My children are both ten. In two months I'm going to have another baby. My husband is a farmer. We have two horses, two cows, and two chickens.

Real Pioneer Diary Entry

Tomorrow is the day we leave for Oregon, the day we gather all our courage, hope and luck and start on the long journey toward our destiny. After many days of arranging, packing and buying we still aren't quite ready for this trip into the depths of danger and darkness, fear and death. All of a sudden I feel like a coward and I want to back out and go back home to Tennessee, but I know it's too late now. We've already traveled for more than two weeks to get here and tomorrow we are leaving. But I trust in God and I believe that He will watch over us.

Mr. Matthew Morris*

Fictional Character's Diary Entry

It sure is good to get our feet on the ground here in Independence Missouri after that long ride on the flatboat. We docked here last Thursday and pitched our tent in a grassy area so the animals have plenty of food for the long trip later. It is so noisy here even in the night. Every minute there is a wagon or boat arriving.

I can't believe how much you can buy here. You can get just about anything. But if you don't keep your head in the game you're likely to get cheated.

In these examples we can see the advantages of having a model. Unquestionably, the second two writings are better than the first. Those writers had the supports of structure, style,

* Pseudonym

and language from the models to draw upon in creating their narratives, which the first writer did not have.

THE POWER OF TOOLS

In this chapter, we have run the gamut of personal narratives. The writers' ages were not the deciding factor in how accomplished the pieces were. What models and teacher instruction were able to do was to bring out of young writers the basic elements of personal narrative mentioned at the beginning of this chapter: story, details, and voice. In the next chapter of this book, I hope to show you how the same elements can also make children's imaginative writing exciting.

CHAPTER 10

Imaginative Writing

maginative stories are what children write when we're not watching. Having been presented with many of these stories over time, I am always amazed by the bits and pieces of traditional and popular literature mixed together into one colorful stew. It's not unusual to find a superhero (really the young writer in disguise), a fairy-tale princess, and a TV detective working together to catch a cartoon animal who's been reviving zombies in the emergency room of a hospital. It's clear that children can draw upon many of the elements of different fictional genres, but it's also clear that they don't know how to sort them out or combine them to make a coherent piece of fiction.

Although the jumble of genres in children's writing doesn't bother me when I read their spare-time efforts, I always expect to see something more polished when imaginative writing is taught in school. Not only do I want the resulting pieces to be true to their roots, I also want plots that don't ramble and solutions to problems that don't depend on magic or a dream.

DEVELOPING CONTEXT

Teaching imaginative writing always begins with reading. Reading experience is the context from which children derive a sense of genre and a fund of background knowledge. Moreover, reading imaginative literature does the best job of familiarizing children with the differences between spoken and written language because the evidence of style and unusual language is so obvious. Where else does a child read or hear "Once upon a time"?

The main lessons of this chapter are really a continuation of the lessons in Chapter 2, only here I focus on the larger patterns of content, structure, and style in writing rather than the smaller ones of repeated words and sentences. We will look at the patterns in fairy tales, legends, and stories that children can use to write imaginative pieces in the classroom.

FAIRY TALES AND FOLK TALES

Plot patterns are more evident in traditional literature than in modern literature, which makes them the best place to begin teaching the art of writing imaginative stories. Fairy tales and folktales use the same few plot patterns over and over, but elaborate them differently. One such pattern is the hero on a quest. We see representations of it in "The Three Little Pigs," "The Three Golden Oranges," "Sir Gawain and the Green Knight," and "The Elephant's Child," to name just a few traditional tales from different times and cultures. Fairy tales also use the same traditional devices to move the action forward, such as the number three. In how many tales are there three brothers/sisters, three tasks/trials, three questions, three desirable objects, three obstacles, or three days/years?

The fact that fairy tales and folktales are so appealing to young children is another reason they are a good place to begin. However, you cannot assume that your students bring enough of that context with them from home. We know that for a variety of reasons many parents of all socioeconomic levels do not read to their children. When it comes to the situation of ELLs, overwork, cultural customs, and/or the lack of English literacy may keep otherwise conscientious parents from reading to their children. Thus, primary-level teachers have to test the waters of their students' knowledge of these tales and expand it by reading new ones and new versions of the familiar ones regularly. They also need to talk about these stories with their students, focusing on the prominent features of each and the similarities and differences from story to story. One first-grade teacher I know read three different versions of "The Little Red Hen" to her class, leading them to see how each one differed from the others. Another primary teacher went even further by dividing her class into small groups that read different fairy tales and made notes on whether certain features, such as a hero or a villain, appeared in them. Using the notes from each group, she prepared a grid with the features listed across the top and the names of fairy tales running down the side. To help you understand how such a grid works, I have included both a full picture of it and a close-up on page 120.

Whether or not you choose to do what these teachers did in developing context, I think that guiding your class through the writing process is a necessary step. The vignette below describes how one second-grade teacher led her mixed-language class through the writing of a group fairy tale after they had read and discussed several such tales.

Sharla Sanford's second graders have been working on a group fairy tale for several days. Before attempting their own story, they had heard some fairy tales read aloud and read more on their own. As they became familiar with the genre, they were able to identify many of its conventions and constructed a chart that listed their findings: hero/heroine, problem, unsuccessful tries to solve the problem, solution, and reward or punishment.

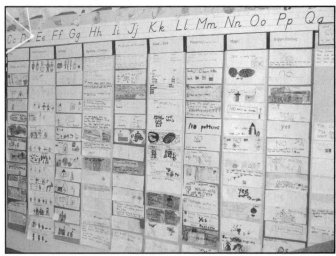

A grid describing features of fairy tales

When the class felt ready to begin its own story, Ms. Sanford had them decide on their characters and make a plan of the plot. The class decided that their major characters would be a king, a queen, and an evil witch. The rest of the characters would be people in the royal court. The plot would involve the kidnapping of the queen and the king's efforts to get her back. Everything would end happily with the queen's return and the witch's punishment.

On the day I visited, the completed parts of the story appeared on five large sheets of chart paper taped to the classroom wall. Scratch-outs and new

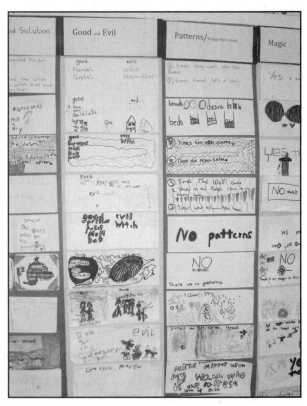

A closer look at parts of the fairy tale grid

words written between the lines showed that many changes had been made as the story progressed. Children who had questions or suggestions about the story as it stood so far had also stuck several sticky notes on the charts. One of the suggestions was that the main characters be given names to help identify them and make them seem more like real people.

Before having the class continue their story, Ms. Sanford had them reread what they had already written. Then children were to discuss with their partners what should happen next. After a few minutes of partner consultation, several children were ready to make suggestions. One child suggested that the palace guards should capture the witch and put her in the dungeon. Another thought that the witch should use her magic wand to hold back the guards and escape. A third child said that the king, disguised as a guard, should grab the witch, take her wand from her, and set the queen free.

The consensus of the class was that the story should go on a while longer, so the witch should not be captured right then. Amalia came up with the following piece of dialogue to continue the story: "Ha, ha, ha," laughed the witch, "the queen will never leave my mansion again." Then Viktor added the words, "You'll never take the queen away from me."

STORIES FOR THE INTERMEDIATE GRADES

By the time students have reached the intermediate grades, they usually consider themselves too old for fairy tales, but they are not too old for traditional stories. They watch them on television and at the movies, and still enjoy hearing them read aloud. But most of the reading they do independently and as class assignments is in modern fiction. The best way to get them into reading and writing traditional stories, may be to embed them in the study of the times and places where they originated. This serves the dual purpose of making the factual content of social studies units come alive and of providing background knowledge about literary genres to give authenticity to their writing.

Of course, many teachers do this already. In Chapter 9, you saw some examples of student writing that came from studying the American western settlement. One sixth-grade teacher I know asks her students to write Chinese proverbs and astrological predictions when they are studying ancient China. Other teachers include trickster tales in the study of Africa.

Native American Legends

For our purposes, Native American legends are a good genre to emphasize because they are part of the study of Native American cultures in the intermediate-level curriculum in most schools. With reading, models, and guided practice, intermediate-level students are able to produce interesting and authentic-sounding pieces. The key features of legends from cultures that did not have science or written literature are supernatural explanations of natural phenomena, such as the seasons of the year. Thus their plots are very simple and almost always the same: Something important in our lives did not always exist or was once very different; here is how supernatural forces created or changed it. The style of Native American legends is also different from other genres. It tends to be spare, respectful, and laced with descriptive names for animals, people, and things. A river might be called "Laughing Water," a person, "Bold Warrior," or a wild pig, "Screeching Forest Runner."

Here are two examples of Native American legends, the first written by a third-grade ELL and the second by a fifth-grade English-speaking student.

How the Beaver Got His Flat Tail

Long, long ago there was a beaver in the path where Native Americans used to walk. One day a Native American stepped on his tail. The beaver said, "Ouch!!"

"One Native American stopped and said to his friends, "Did you hear that?" They looked and looked. They wondered, "Who said ouch?"

The Beaver said, "Down here. You stepped on my tail that I use for building my houses and dams and made it flat."

The Native Americans picked the beaver up and said, "We are sorry for stepping on your tail. Is there anything we can do that will make you happy?"

The beaver said, "Okay. Take me to your village and give me some sticks to build my house." They did.

That is why beavers have flat tails.

—by Anthony

How Horses Got Their Markings

Many moons ago there was a herd of horses. Teayas the stallion, who was the leader of the herd, was taking them south to find more food. But Teayas did not know that the herd was heading straight for a huge prairie fire. By the time he sensed the fire, it had spread all around them. Teayas did not waste his time. He immediately gathered the herd around him and told them that the only way out was through the fire. Teayas and the other horses ran right through the flames. Ever since that time, horses have always had a flame marking on the back of their necks and on their tails.

Native American Prayers

Along with legends, religious invocations were part of Native American cultures. People prayed to various gods for help in many situations where they had no control, such as drought, war, and disease. One teacher embedded animal prayers in a unit on preserving the world's eco-systems. Although the primary purpose of having students write the following prayers was to have them learn about animals' environmental needs, the teacher also showed them models of Native American prayers and asked them to use their traditional features.

Prayer of the Frog

Dear Spirit,

Thank you for the foolish fly, the big fat mosquito, and other bugs I snatch with my tongue. Please help change the diet of the snakes and blue herons, as it now includes me. Also keep the ponds and other water places clean and safe from pollution. Bless all amphibians, especially those that croak.

Prayer of the Mink

Dear Mother Nature,

Today I didn't scare anyone, and I never hunt unless I'm hungry. Thank you for my rich, thick fur that keeps me warm, and for all the crayfish and muskrats you provide for me.

Why do people always try to get my fur? Help me avoid their traps. Please, Mother Nature, protect me and all animal kind.

WRITING IN TRADITIONAL GENRES

In addition to writing about America, elementary-level students could be doing more writing in other literary genres from other times and places, such as fables, myths, animal tales, tall tales, trickster tales, and moral tales. I will present three examples of these genres in my collection of children's writings here. I have chosen to include these examples because they were all written by second graders whose teacher exposed them to a wide range of literary genres through reading aloud and having them read simple models.

Although the first example is clearly a legend in form, it seems very modern. It does not have any of the cultural characteristics that the ones presented earlier display.

Legend

Before the bald eagle got his haircut, he was called a "hairy eagle." When he saw his friend the lion getting a haircut, he wanted a haircut, too. He went and told his mother. She gave him some money for a haircut.

On the way to the barbershop he got hungry, so he spent all his money on candy. He went and told his mother what he did. She gave him some more money.

He went to the barbershop and told the barber to cut off a little on the sides. The barber cut it all off accidentally. That's how the bald eagle got bald.

Tall Tale

One day Paul Bunyan was taking a walk. He was just about to pick a flower when he heard a crack. It came from up above. Paul Bunyan wanted to know what it was so he walked on to the top of the tallest mountain. He saw that the earth's ring had broken, so he bought some Super Glue and glued it back together. Then he noticed that Mars looked a bit dull so he got a lot of metal and made a ring for Mars.

Fable

One day, on February 2nd, a groundhog woke up and looked out of his hole and said, "I don't see anything but clouds." He caught sight of a snake and asked the snake, "Are you hungry?" The snake said, "Yes." Do you want to have breakfast with me?" asked the groundhog. "Sure," said the snake. So the snake ate up the groundhog.

The moral: Don't have any meals with your enemy.

To introduce your students to legends, fables, myths, or tall tales from various cultures, you can go to any of the following sources. They, in turn, will lead you to others.

Just So Stories by Rudyard Kipling
The Jungle Book by Rudyard Kipling

Anansi and the Box of Stories by Stephen Krensky

Uncle Remus: His Songs and His Sayings by Joel Chandler Harris

American Tall Tales by Mary Pope Osborne

D'Aulaires' Book of Norse Myths by Ingri and Edgar Parson d'Aulaire

IMAGINATIVE STORIES

We come finally to the field of contemporary stories. Unfortunately, as I said at the beginning of this chapter, it is not a productive area for elementary-level writers. For the most part teachers don't touch it, probably because they sense its pitfalls. The closest they seem to come is asking students to write stories based on literature they've read. In Chapter 9, you saw three personal narratives inspired by the book *Alexander and the Terrible, Horrible, No Good, Very Bad Day* and one derived from the fairy tale "Little Red Riding Hood." But even with good models such as these, many young writers have problems. They often put too much dialogue into their stories and not enough description or action. They also rush their plots to a conclusion, as if they have grown bored with the whole thing. Knowing children, I suspect they do get bored when any piece of writing takes up too much of their valuable time.

A Story Strategy

What can teachers do about these problems? They can make the experience more structured, more exciting, and shorter. In the vignette below, we see the instructional process of one teacher who manages to keep her students engaged in writing stories.

> In Emma Harris's grades 1–2 mixed-language classroom, children are creating imaginative stories based on an elaborate design on an antique Blue Willow plate. After examining the design of the plate yesterday, the children brainstormed possible plots, characters, actions, and settings for their stories Then Ms. Harris modeled her own way of "pulling out" a story from the design by choosing a bluebird as her main character and the problem of where it should build its nest as the key to the plot. She told the class the beginning of her story and stopped there. Afterward she asked each child to imagine the basic outlines of his or her own story and tell it to a partner. Then Ms. Harris modeled making a sectioned planning sheet for her story and set the class to work sketching their stories into the sections as they told it again.

Today Ms. Harris begins the lesson by gathering the children on the classroom rug and showing the story she has sketched out. As she points to each drawing on her planning sheet, she tells the story she has in her head—episode by episode—about a bluebird, its eggs, and a predatory snake. She begins by saying, "One day," pointing out to the children that these words are often used to start a story.

When Ms. Harris has finished telling her story, she asks the children to suggest a title for it. After taking several suggestions, she decides on "The Bluebird and the Snake." With a different colored pencil than she used yesterday—to distinguish today's additions from her original drawings—she writes the title in the first section of her planning sheet. Then, using the colored pencil again, she adds details to each drawing.

After adding details to describe what the characters might be seeing, hearing, smelling, touching, tasting, or feeling emotionally, she instructs the class about their task for the day, which is to do with their own stories what she has modeled, also using a different colored pencil from the one they used yesterday. Before adding details, however, the children should tell their stories once again to the person opposite them at their tables and ask for questions and suggestions. After adding their details, they are to tell their stories one more time to a new partner. Finally, they will cut apart their planning sheets and paste their drawings in blank notebooks, one to a page. Tomorrow they will write their stories, "pulling the events out" for episodes to put in the spaces below each drawing.

All the children set to work eagerly while Ms. Harris moves around the room offering help. After almost an hour of steady work, she calls a break for those who need one, and offers a choice of new activities. But she also allows children who are still interested in working on their stories to continue writing.

Emma Harris's instructional process moves me to remind you of the importance of using partners in teaching all kinds of imaginative writing. This strategy pushes writers to think through the totality of their stories, to include important details, and to use clear language. Teachers should demonstrate and give guided practice on the role of being a partner early in the year and review it from time to time, reminding students that a good partner lets a writer know when he or she needs to change or add to the story.

To see how well Ms. Harris's students learned from her instruction let's look at one story written by a first-grade ELL. I have left her invented spellings as they appeared in her final version, which was bound into an illustrated booklet.

> One day, a Sunday, a bird came. He saw a bitful tree. He decided to build his nest in the bitful tree. So he did. Then he flew off the tree. He picked up some grass to make the nest warm.
>
> The first bird met another bird. The first bird said, "were will we put are nest?"
>
> "Let's go to the magic house. We will find a tree."
>
> "I foud a tree to build are nest. Look at this tree."
>
> They lay eggs. One egg! Two eggs! Then another egg. Three eggs. There were 5 eggs. They have 5 eggs. The birds flew. The babies went first. The mother went next. The duck was getting water. The man duck put his beak in the bird food. And the birds had a bitful house.
>
> —By Ana

Outside of not making clear who said the lines and not explaining what the "magic house" was, Ana wrote a complete and coherent story that stays within its genre. The strategy her teacher used of having the children tell and draw their stories, encouraging them to develop a plot thoroughly, and include visual details worked for most of these young writers. She also discouraged excessive dialogue. Moreover, the story length was manageable for ELLs who are just beginning to learn to express themselves in written English.

BOOK REPORTS

Although most teachers would expect to find book reports in the chapter on academic writing, I have chosen to put them here. The problem is that the traditional book report was never meant to be a piece of writing; it is a test of whether students have read and understood the books they claim to have read. Given that rationale, why have teachers always asked for book reports rather than giving a test? The answer is that it's too difficult to design tests for all the books students might read—although a commercial publisher has done just that and is being paid very well for those tests. So in most cases the burden of proof is passed from the teacher to the student in the form of an assigned written book report. From a student's point of view, nothing could be more meaningless and more onerous than writing a book report. But he has no choice; he writes the report. The teacher reads it and grades it, and everyone is relieved until the next book report comes along.

One remedy is to replace the traditional book report with a brief imaginative writing that serves the original purpose while being fun to write and interesting to read. I'm going to offer three possible forms—although I'm sure there are more. Intermediate-level students should be able to do any of the three; primary-level students would probably do best with the personal narrative/letter form.

Cinquain Book Report

Ramona

Annoying, troublesome

Argues, jabbers, bothers

Embarrasses people

Ramona.

—from the book, *Ramona and Beezus*

News Article Book Report

MOUSE INVADES INVENTOR'S SHOP

(Philadelphia, PA)

Late last night a small mouse, identified as Amos, left his large family in the church to seek his fortune. Some witnesses say that he knocked on many doors, but when the residents opened the door they saw nothing there. Of course, they might have if they had looked down.

When Amos reached the home of the great Benjamin Franklin, he slipped in as it seemed he'd have many interesting things to explore.

Perhaps a mousetrap will end Amos' journey. To track down the end of this story, read . . . *Ben and Me* by Robert Lawson

Letter Book Report

Dear Reader,

I live in an old farmhouse with my grandpa, brother and sister. Oh, and then there's our dog, Mud. I am an inventor and I just invented a coyote trap. I'm going to win a hundred dollars for catching a coyote.

I didn't want anyone to see my test trap so I left with my dog, Mud, to set my trap in the woods. I crawled into my trap to bait it, and the door shut on me. I built that trap so strong, I knew I'd never get it open.

I cried myself to sleep from frustration. I just woke up and I'm not in the trap. I'm in a cave and sitting in a rocking chair is a witch!

How did I get here? What will she do to me? Will someone find me? If so, when?

Sincerely,
Junior Blossom

—from *The Blossoms Meet the Vulture Lady* by Betsy Byars

FINAL THOUGHTS

Throughout this chapter, I kept wishing I could show you more examples of children's imaginative writing, but I did not have them. Nevertheless, I do not accept the premise that children cannot write stories, legends, myths, folktales, and other forms of imaginative writing. Can it be that the overemphasis on testing and test preparation in schools today has squeezed out imaginative writing along with art, music, and physical education? Or even worse, is it possible that the current view of education as cramming the largest possible quantity of information and the greatest number of mechanical skills into students' heads has left no room for children to read authentic literature or for teachers to motivate them to write their own?

CHAPTER 11

Poetry

After lamenting the scarcity of imaginative writing in elementary classrooms, I am happy to report that poetry is plentiful. Somehow this form strikes teachers as a type of writing they should teach, perhaps because children like poetry or perhaps because stories are long and poems are short. Actually, I suspect a different reason entirely: tradition. High-quality poetry has been a part of the language arts curriculum in elementary schools for a long time, while high-quality prose has not. Only in the past 30 years have we seen an explosion of good children's novels and short stories in schools.

Because writing poetry is more difficult than writing prose, I am also happy to see how well children do with it. Unlike prose, whose only requirement is adherence to the particular genre chosen, poetry has four basic elements: rhythm, precision, economy, and symmetry. Most of the children's poetry I've seen has at least two of those elements, indicating that the young writers have grasped the concept of what a poem is—and that is remarkable.

Before getting into the teaching of poetry let me define what I have called its basic elements, so you can look for them in the poems presented in this chapter. *Rhythm* is the sound pattern made by the sequence of syllables and silences in a poem's structure. *Precision* is the selection of words that best fit a poem's meaning and its rhythm. *Economy* means that a good poem does not have extra words; each word does its job, and some words do double duty. And *symmetry* is the design formed by the repetition or relatedness of words, sounds, and ideas throughout the poem.

EARLY POEMS

Most of the early poems that children write are highly imitative, using a published poem's form and language, and substituting only a few new words for the original ones. Although we cannot properly call imitative poetry original writing, I consider imitation an acceptable and useful support for children who are just getting into poetry or just learning English. Not only does imitation familiarize children with the forms and elements of poetry, it also builds their vocabulary and knowledge of sentence structure.

When a child chooses to imitate a poem he likes, I would encourage him to make it as different as possible from the original by picking a completely new topic. But I must admit that it's hard to get children to make such a large change. If a poem is about one animal and what it does, most children will just name a new animal and some new actions. Since some imitative poems were presented in Chapter 2, I will show only two more here. I chose these because the young poets did make real changes in their poems' content. Still, I think you will recognize their sources. The first poem was written by a second-grade boy, the second by a fourth-grade girl.

Little Billy Dilly
    was eating some chili,
    was eating some chili quite hot.
Said he, "It doesn't matter
    how much I get fatter
    I'm just a little person after all."

******

Twinkle, twinkle, satellite,
How I wonder why you're bright!
Up above the world so high
Like a firecracker in the sky.

FINDING RHYMES

For young children poetry means rhyme, since they haven't yet met any blank verse or free verse, and they wouldn't call that poetry if they had. Even when children are not imitating a particular poem, they try to write poems like the ones they know. Too often, unfortunately, they can't think of rhyming words that make sense and, therefore, wind up with something silly. To help children find appropriate rhymes, I suggest setting up a worksheet that lists all the letters of the alphabet (except Q and X) down the side, with spaces for the words they want rhymes for across the top. The idea is to write a "target" word in the top space, then go through the alphabet sounds and list all the words you can think of that rhyme with the target. Most of the time, children can find one or more words that will work, but if they can't, they need to choose a different target word.

Even in the intermediate grades some students, especially ELLs, may have trouble with rhymes. Recently I tried to teach limericks to a fourth-grade, mixed-language class that had had a unit on poetry in third grade. I thought they would like the humor and the strong rhythm of this form. They did, but they couldn't write their own limericks, even with specific instruction from their teacher and me. Although my analysis of the problem may be self-serving, I concluded that these students had not had sufficient context building before or during my lessons. Not only were they not familiar with limericks, they didn't know much about rhymes. And, in preparing my lessons, I did not know enough about their skills or their previous experience with poetry. I don't think the students' difficulties were connected to second-language learning, since none of them were newcomers, and most of them wrote well enough in prose.

PRODUCING RHYTHM

A second problem for young poets is getting the right number of syllables into a line. I am not suggesting that children should write in iambic pentameter, but they do have to write lines of similar metric length to achieve some reasonable rhythm in a poem. To make children aware of rhythm, teachers can have them clap through real poems or recite nonsense words (e.g., ta-da-da, ta-da-da, ta-da for the first line of a limerick) to match a poem's syllables. They will see that each line has the same, or nearly the same, number of claps or "ta-das." When they are writing their own poems, they need to test its rhythm using the same process, alone or with a partner's help.

Below is a poem by a seven-year-old native English speaker that has both rhyme and meter. I decided to include it because it is such an exception in my collection of young children's poetry. We could say that finding rhymes was just a matter of luck for this child, but her careful use of meter looks deliberate to me.

I have a mitten
I have a blouse
I've got a kitten
Inside my house.

I realize that the suggestions I've given for teaching rhyme and meter assume that your students know the phonemes for all letters and can segment words. In primary-level classes, especially mixed-language ones, this may not be true. If that is the case, go through the demonstration and whole-class activities anyway, give individual help to those who need it, and joyfully accept whatever flawed efforts you get. In these circumstances, you may not be teaching poetry as much as you are teaching reading. So be it!

PATTERNED POEMS

The best poems I've seen from primary-level children are pattern-based ones that may or may not rhyme. To write them, children borrow patterns from published poems but use their own ideas for the content. Below is an excerpt from a poem by two second-grade girls who used a familiar counting pattern as a framework for their own ideas. The second poem may or may not be a borrowed pattern; I don't know. Either way, I think it is a remarkable accomplishment for a girl who was only eight years old.

Ten little pumpkins
Sitting on the vine.
One was chosen
Now there are nine.

Nine little pumpkins
Stayed out so late
One overslept
So now there are eight.

******

Cat and bat in a witch's brew
With a witch saying, "Hackity-boo."
Flies from France
Ants from pants
Spiders black
Butterflies blue
Mix them in the magic brew.
Crunchy and munchy for witches and wizards.
Add ghosts, old creaky creatures, mummies for fun
Now my witch's brew is done.

The fourth-grade, mixed-language class I mentioned earlier that had trouble writing limericks was able to produce some good pattern-based poems. Two ELLs from that class wrote poems based on the pattern "Come See What I Found" by Kristine O'Connell George. At right are their poems and drawings, with the original spelling and punctuation preserved.

A poem by Jonathan, a fourth grader

FIXED-FORM POETRY

Intermediate-level teachers often choose to teach traditional fixed-form poems to show their students how important form is. One popular fixed form is the haiku, which has three lines, the first with five syllables, the second with seven, and the third with five again. The context for the haiku is fairly simple to build, if you don't get into the Japanese roots of the form. Another form, the cinquain, has five lines, with one word each in the first and last lines and two, three, and four words in the sec-

A poem by Lupita, a fourth grader

TEACHING WRITING IN MIXED-LANGUAGE CLASSROOMS

ond, third and fourth lines, respectively. A third form is the triplet, which, as its name implies, has three lines. Its only requirements are that the lines all be about the same length and that they can be sensibly read in any order. Some young poets are even able to make them rhyme.

In teaching these forms, teachers should have students study models, talk about their features, brainstorm possible topics, and then try to write them. Poetry is the one area where there is usually no group writing, probably because the impulse to write poetry and the approach to any particular poem are so individual. But teachers do spend a significant amount of time with each student, discussing word choices and questioning tone and line length. Here are examples of all three forms written by fourth and fifth graders.

Haiku

The acacia trees
Show black against the sunset
On the savannah

Triplets

How absurd
That rainbow parrot bird
It cannot speak a word

Cinquain

Ghouls
Thrilling, chilling
Looming, glooming, dooming
Slimy, grimy
Ghouls

FREE VERSE

Outside of the three traditional fixed forms I have just described, most of the poetry taught at the intermediate level is free verse. Teachers often initiate the writing of free verse by examining a real poem, reading a story, or viewing a picture. One teacher I know likes to use a poem by William Carlos Williams, entitled "This Is Just to Say." Following Williams's poem is a student poem modeling it.

This Is Just to Say

I have eaten
the plums
that were in
the icebox

And which
you were probably
saving
for breakfast

Forgive me
they were delicious
so sweet
and so cold

      ******

Stacey and I
played a great game
of Nintendo
I was just
about to win

When you called
to remind me
about taping your
T.V. show

Forgive me
for forgetting to
do it.
I was busy winning my game.

Intermediate students take to free verse readily because it does not demand rhyme or rhythm. As its name implies, this form of poetry frees writers to concentrate on precision and economy and include common features of poetry, such as visual images, memories, and emotions. You will see these features in the examples of free verse that follow.

COLOR POEMS

The most commonly used free verse stimulus—at both the intermediate and primary levels—is a categorical word, such as *summer*, *friendship*, *family*, *snow*, or *school*. These words bring many childhood experiences and feelings to the surface. *Color* is also a favorite and fruitful stimulus. Teachers ask children to write poems that are a series of statements about how a particular color makes them feel. In addition to models, this kind of poem requires instruction and guided practice because young writers are not used to matching a feeling to a color. The easy part is choosing the color they want to write about. The hard parts are figuring out the mood that color suggests to them and then finding specific things that fit that mood and that color. Below are two examples, the first by a first grader and the second by a fifth grader. Notice that the first grader's choices of blue things have nothing to do with mood, while the intermediate writer has not only matched a mood to the color and chosen objects that reflect that mood, but has also taken on the further challenge of making her poem rhyme, so it is not actually a free verse poem.

What is blue?
My sweatshirt is blue.
The sea is blue
A blue jay is blue.
The sky is blue
The blue whale is blue.
The earth is blue
The color blue is blue.

******

Gray is a rain cloud,
A loaf of stale bread,
Smoke and ashes,
A day that you dread.
Tin cans and trash cans are gray.

Wads of gum, too,

Cold potatoes, fog,

And a worn-out shoe.

The feeling of gray is sad

Like a drizzly day,

When nobody has anything

Right to say.

PERSONAL EXPERIENCE POEMS

At the intermediate level, teachers may encourage students to write about something in their personal experience that piqued their interest or stirred their feelings. For these poems, there is no class instruction. They represent individual imagination and verbal ability. Here are poems that grades 4–5 students wrote on their own.

The Brave Deer

He snorts and threatens

He drives them away.

Challenging buck after buck,

Shoving with neck power,

He guards his mate.

It's time for finding food.

He peels off bark,

Paws for sweet grass in the snow,

Cracks fallen acorns,

And chews at tender twigs.

Then finds a safe place to rest.

He is satisfied.

The Rocking Chair

Out there on the porch I see the rocking chair

With a slight Kansas wind blowing,

Making it rock.

I seem to picture it saying,
"Come, come and rock on me,
Please, won't someone rock on me?"

It looked so sad.
I could tell it wanted someone,
Maybe a grandma or a grandpa
Or maybe just some little kid
Making the rocking chair
Go like crazy.

I left that Kansas wind
And soon grew old,
Old enough to sit in that rocking chair
And sway back and forth whenever I wanted to.
I did this mostly though
For the rocking chair.

The Loss of a Friend

My kite just dove and crashed in the treetops.
It looks like it's broke—a goner I think.
I loved that kite; I called her Ophelia
Her body was purple; her tail was hot pink.

I have possessed her for over a year now.
I bought her in Shopko the first day of fall.
She's flown very well, riding high when twas windy.
Now I cannot fly Ophelia at all.

It looks like she's breaking away from the treetop.
She's pulling away with a wish for the sky.
Pop! Her string broke; at last she has freedom.
Now I must whisper a dear friend goodbye.

What is most interesting to me in these original poems are things their teachers didn't teach: breaking lines in unexpected places—as thoughts or a voice might break—mood and tone. I think that because these young writers had assimilated much of poetry's basic nature through a generous exposure over time, they were able to infuse it unconsciously into their writing.

LIMITATIONS OF POETRY

In this chapter I have displayed a lot of children's poetry, but said little about teaching it. That is because outside of imitative poetry and fixed-form poetry, there is not much one can teach. What the teachers of these young poets did was to expose their students to different kinds of poems regularly and to point out their features, especially the elements of rhythm and symmetry. They really could not emphasize economy because their students would have thought they meant that all poems should be short. In private consultations, teachers focused on precision by questioning uninteresting and overused words and encouraging their students to find just the right words for their poems. But it is clear from looking at the range of poems I have presented, that many children, especially ELLs, do not have enough synonyms under their control to make nuanced choices.

As I said earlier, I think several of the poems I've shown are remarkable considering the ages of the students who wrote them. Will any of these students become professional poets? Who knows? I feel more confident in predicting that many of them will become strong writers in all the areas they choose to write in.

The Last Word

As I wrote the various chapters of this book, I found myself going back frequently to earlier chapters to make changes. Those changes were not to correct errors in writing, but to alter my original thinking. Simply put, I had changed my mind. In a very real sense, I learned as I wrote, seeing more deeply into the complexity of teaching writing and the difficulties young writers face when learning to write. The key factor in my learning was my continuing visits to classrooms. All these classrooms were in schools where most of the students were ELLs, and the few native English speakers were poor. There was also a high student turn-over. Often when I went back to a classroom and asked about a student I had been interested in, the teacher replied, "She moved away."

Before getting to know these classrooms and these students, all my experience, both as a teacher and a principal, had been in upper-middle-class schools where students stayed put for five or six years and, more important, where educated parents had been enriching their children's lives with books, educational trips, and dinnertime conversation. Most of those students wrote easily and knowledgeably in any form their teachers asked for. They had no trouble seeing the conventions that characterized a type of writing and infusing them into their own pieces in creative ways. No matter what anyone says about the responsibility of schools to close the achievement gap, I believe that the socioeconomic differences among students have a powerful and unyielding impact on academic success.

What I began to see once I went into high-poverty schools was that many children found writing difficult. Yes, they had learned how to spell, punctuate, and write grammatically correct sentences, but they still had a hard time writing original work or conforming to the conventions of various forms of writing. I also saw that most teachers were working very hard at teaching writing, but to little effect. The writing they wanted was beyond their students' experience with books and their lives outside of school. Given the particular needs of their students, the methods and materials teachers were using did not offer the right kinds of support.

Even before my school visits, I knew that all children need models they can imitate, modify, or use as springboards for their own writing. What I didn't know was how much children from diverse backgrounds also need context and guidance throughout the writing process because they may not have travelled down those literary roads before. Teachers' and peers' advice about revising first drafts is of little help when writers have already made wrong turns and stumbled into potholes.

And so this book developed with the repeated emphasis on context, models, and in-process guidance. The types of writing suggested are relatively short, well-defined in form, and with a clear trajectory. Although I certainly would not discourage any young writer from exploring the uncharted territories of modern stories and rhymed poetry, I would not present those forms as class assignments.

My closing advice to the teachers who have stayed with me through this book is to reread its introduction. This is the part of the book I changed the most as I wrote new chapters; hence it reflects my best thinking about teaching and the needs of elementary-level students. Above all, read again and be heartened by the last tenet of my writing philosophy:

Learning to write well is a lifelong journey. Each small step taken along the way is a worthy accomplishment.

Index